# PUT
# YOUR
# MOTHER
# ON
# THE
# CEILING

# PUT YOUR MOTHER ON THE CEILING

## Richard de Mille

A PUBLICATION OF THE GESTALT JOURNAL PRESS

*To*

*Tony*

*who started off with*

*a levitation machine*

*and Cecil*

*who said, "That's crazy!*

*You can't walk through*

*a tree trunk."*

# CONTENTS

# Preface
## to the
## Gestalt Journal Press Edition

Imagination is the essence of creative living, but it has not always been appreciated. During World War I, Carl Gustav Jung wrote: "Imagination . . . has a poor reputation among psychologists, and [up to now] psychoanalytic theories have treated it accordingly" (Jung 1956, 298). Jung valued dreams and daydreams as a means of growth and self-discovery. In contrast, both Freud and the behaviorists depreciated imagination. Freud took fantasies to be a sign of neurosis. Unhappy people imagined things; happy people stuck to reality. The behaviorists in their laboratories brushed imagination aside as something superficial. Rats running in mazes were real; imagination existed only in the imagination.

Nevertheless, an early therapeutic use of imagination grew out of animal experiments. Joseph Wolpe taught some cats to fear an object in the laboratory. Then he removed their fear by bringing them in small, painless steps closer and closer to the feared object. This was called systematic desensitization.* Applying the same principle to human beings, he was able to relieve irrational fears (of spiders, kittens, supermarkets, or whatever it might be) by asking the fearful person to *imagine* coming closer a little at a time to what he was afraid of. Wolpe's therapeutic success surprised his fellow behaviorists, who had believed that thoughts did not cause anything to happen; they were mere reflections of what happened, having no power of their own. Wolpe's discovery that imagining would change timid behavior raised an old philosophical question: do thoughts merely reflect what happens in the world, or do they also change what happens? Common experience suggests it goes both ways. The world around us changes our thoughts, and our thoughts, by changing our behavior, change the world around us. Thoughts are both effects and causes. Wolpe was not the first to apply this principle. Some years earlier, Frederick Perls had used visualization exercises to change behavior (Perls 1992; Perls et al. 1994).

In writing this book, I made three assumptions. First, I assumed that thoughts are as real as overt acts; the two are different, of course, but both are real; we really act, and we really

---

* Wolpe's method included other elements, notably systematic relaxation (Rachman 1967), but Wilkins (1971) calls instructed imagination the only necessary element. Though Wolpe named his imagery technique "behavior therapy," Locke (1971) said it contradicted major premises of behaviorism. For a general discussion of directed imagery, see Singer (1971).

have thoughts. Next, I assumed that thoughts can change feelings and behavior. Third, I assumed that we don't have to wait for dreams or daydreams to occur but can ask people to imagine particular things. When I wrote the first version of these games, in 1954, such assumptions were out of favor in psychology, but today they are widely applied in psychotherapy and teaching. In the directed daydream technique (Hammer 1967; Johnsgard 1969), the therapist suggests key features of a visual fantasy, and the client fills in the details. The therapist may ask the client to take a journey through his body, telling what is found there, or to confront figures seen in a recurring nightmare, or to imagine dealing with a parent or a boss. Confronting frightening figures, feeding powerful giants, and making friends with hostile beings are frequently used fantasies. Imaginary locations include house, meadow, mountain, cave, forest, and ocean bottom. The reader will find similar elements in this book.

As useful as they are in therapy, imagination exercises work even better in education. The games give practice in visualization and teach children to distinguish fantasy from reality. They make children (and adults) more comfortable with their bodies and their private thoughts. They show that the thinker is the master, thoughts are the servants — not the other way round. Children often believe that ideas have magical power: If I think a bad thought, a bad thing will happen. The games teach that this is not so. Magic works in stories; life requires practical actions. Because people sometimes fear that their thoughts will run away with them, I wrote a set of instructions for getting rid of persistent images. An idea you can't get out of your head is *made* to occur in many different forms, until it is under your control and comes or goes according to your wishes. In psychology, this has been called negative practice.*

In recent years fantasy has been recognized as a useful and necessary part of normal living (Klinger 1971; Sheehan 1972; Singer 1966). Research has found that creative persons have easy access to their private imagery (Dellas & Gaier 1970; Sheehan 1966). Persons who perceive the world accurately are likely to possess vivid imagery. Persons who are willing to engage in fantasy understand themselves better, distinguish fantasy from reality better, and are less disconcerted by unexpected thoughts and images. They also have more fun. We are now ready, it seems, to do something for the little boy who told his teacher he couldn't concentrate because his imagination kept getting into fights with his mind (Brown 1990, 231). In an early test of the games in this book, first-graders became more confident of their own thinking by learning that imagining doesn't have to follow the rules of reality. We don't need scuba gear to imagine walking on the bottom of the ocean, though we would need it to walk

---

* A person can change a habit by practicing both the desired and the undesired form of it (Dunlap 1932). The same principle is implied in discussions of rubricizing (Maslow 1954) and subsidiary awareness (Polanyi 1964).

there in reality. Teacher Gloria Castillo told what happened in the classroom.*

During three months, I read the games in order. Many children responded by making up their own games. In discussions afterwards, some would bring up things that were bothering them. This helped me to understand, and sometimes alleviate, fears or difficulties that were interfering with learning. Often, at a child's request, we would repeat a game. Afterwards, the child who had asked to play the game again would seem calmer and less anxious. If a child was edgy or out of sorts, I would hand him the book and ask if he wanted to play one of the games. Usually he would choose one, and we would all play it. Most of the children could find their way around in the book without any help. In summary, I would say I used the book in the first grade as a story to develop listening skills, as a stimulus to imagination, as a language developer, as a story model, as a way to write, and as a tool for dealing with the

---

* Gloria Castillo. "Eight months in the first grade" (In Brown 1990, 113-165), letter to RdeM.

children's concerns. No wonder I kept it so handy and recommended it to so many teachers!

*Put Your Mother on the Ceiling* was the first book of its kind, a set of mental exercises disguised as entertainments for children and their parents or teachers. Over the years it has been commended, quoted* and imitated.** The renowned educational psychologist J. P. Guilford said:

> The games should help the child to be more flexible in thinking and more generally creative. They should promote better control of imagination, so that it can be turned on and off as needed. By calling attention to differences between what is imagined and what is actual, the games should extend and protect the child's capacity for rational living.

In the next section Professor Guilford's systematic analysis of intelligence will help us understand Why We Should

---

\* Adams (1976, 60-61); Bry & Bair (1978, 128,164); Castillo (1974, 82-85,221); Joan T. Freyberg (in Singer 1973, 132); McKim (1972, 99-102,111)); Mary Ann Pulaski (in Singer 1973, 76,103); Singer (1971; 1973, 244-245,254; 1975, 242-245); Yawkey & others (1981).
\*\* Readers of Aldous Huxley's novel *Island* (1962, 262) will discover when playing the game "Animals" that its mice were turned by Huxley into one-legged mynah birds for his Palinese children. Huxley (in Farber & Wilson 1961, 71) called the games "a catalyst for the imagination . . . enormous fun and practical teaching aids."

Put Mother on the Ceiling (Guilford, 1967). Mental capacity and intellectual performance are today not simply academic topics; they have become socially controversial. Parents and teachers want to know what they can do to promote learning and improve the lives of children and adults beyond what may be predicted by an IQ score. Playing imagination games is one thing we can do to free the mind of a child and make him or her more creative, more effective, happier, and more successful.

*Richard de Mille*
*Santa Barbara, May 1997*

# WHY
# WE
# SHOULD
# PUT
# MOTHER
# ON
# THE
# CEILING

There seems to be a permanent war going on between reality and imagination. The battleground is childhood. On the side of imagination we have the child, eyes great with wonder, mouth issuing fantasies, misconceptions, and unreliable reports. Parents, teachers, the peer group, and the police are on the side of reality. They keep insisting on truth, accuracy, conformity, and obedience.

Sometimes the fight is fierce. *Make up another story like that and I'll tell your father.* But at other times it is just a holding action. *Don't sit there dreaming — get your clothes on.* Occasionally we negotiate. *Never mind the pillow fairy. Give me the tooth and take the dollar.*

*Stop the War*

This is not a war to take sides in, because there is much to be said on either side. The main purpose of putting Mother on the ceiling is to stop the war, so that reality and imagination can live in harmony.

The demands of growing up put a premium on realism. The world is a complicated, difficult, often dangerous place. Parents want children — especially their own children, whom they love very much — to be able to understand it, cope with it, and survive in it. They know that a realistic attitude can be a great help, and they work hard teaching children to recognize what is fact and what is fiction.

2  *Why*

There is no need (Mother points out) to exaggerate. *Daddy didn't chase the burglar. He just called the police.* Imaginary playmates do not rate full privileges. *I'm not setting any place for Charlie Brown — or for Snoopy either.* Stories are just stories. *It's too hot at the center of the earth. No one can go there.* The dark won't hurt you. *See? It's not a bear, it's a chair. When I turn the light off again, it will still be a chair.*

Wouldn't it be fun if stories were true, Daddy were a hero, and we could know comic-strip people! On the other hand, it is a good thing the furniture remains harmless while we are sleeping.

Distinctions between reality and imagination are necessary, and it is important that they be learned. But it is also important to teach the distinctions in a way that does not turn off the imagination.

A human being may be taught to give exactly right answers to thousands of questions, as a computer may be programmed to give the location of any item in a warehouse or to compute interest on savings for any day in the year. The recall of facts and the calculation of right answers are indispensable in the conduct of daily life, and the schools would be negligent if they did not urge youngsters to master them. But such skills are only part of what a child should learn.

Good judgment, originality, fluency and flexibility of thought, the ability to redefine situations or see their implications — such qualities are prized in human society. In everyday life, they reap rewards of wealth, responsibility, or prestige. In times of peril, they may determine who will survive and who will not. Teaching these abilities should be a major purpose of education.

Contemporary research has shed new light on these neglected mental skills, and this better theoretical understanding is helping educators to place an appropriate emphasis on productive and evaluative thinking. J. P. Guilford's theory called the Structure of Intellect subsumes most of these neglected skills under two formal headings: *divergent production* and *evaluation*.

## Divergent Production

The main difference between divergent production and other kinds of thinking is that it involves the production by the thinker of a *quantity* or *variety* of ideas. The detective who asks himself, "Where did Phil Pickpurse hide those jewels?" must come up with some likely hiding places. All of his ideas must be appropriate. If his ideas are arbitrary or ridiculous, he will waste a lot of time looking where the jewels could not possibly be. But only one of his ideas is likely to be *right*. Rightness is not important in the kind of thinking we call divergent production. Appropriateness, quantity, and variety are important.

Divergent production results when the doctor asks himself, "What are the diseases that show this particular symptom?" The law student, taking his examination, needs it to list all the laws that could apply to a particular dispute. At the factory, the engineer says, "What can we make automobiles out of now?" Across town the junk dealer is thinking, "Now what can we make out of automobiles?"

The mystery writer asks himself, "What are the fifty tight spots Mike Rake will get himself into in my next book?" And the politician sharpens his pencil to list the many disasters that will surely befall his fair and sovereign state if a certain obviously unqualified candidate of the other party is elected.

Mother herself is familiar with two recurring questions of this kind. One is the child's question: "What can I play now?" The other is her own question: "What can we have for dinner?"

The menu planner has great need for divergent production. When she sits down, pencil in hand, numerous animal and vegetable thoughts should flow through her mind. Only with a variety of good possibilities will she be able to plan for each day, not *the* good dinner, but *a* good dinner that has not been served recently. Menu planning is creative work. All creative work depends in part on divergent production.

## Perry at West Point

Divergent production can be taught at school. To take an example from the field of history or social studies, Matthew Perry's visits to Japan in the 1850s are said to have brought Japan into the modern world. In less than a century, Japan changed from a predominantly feudal agricultural society into an industrial power that could challenge the most powerful nation on earth, both in commercial trade and in land, sea, and air warfare. The student may be aware of the events of World War II and may understand that Japan was not one of the very first industrial nations, but will he grasp the significance of Perry's mission?

The teacher has a choice. He can, on the one hand, tell his students that Perry's insistence on negotiating a treaty changed the histories of Japan and the United States. The students may remember that or they may forget it, but either way they will not have had much practice in thinking. On the other hand, suppose the teacher says "What would have happened if, in 1808, Perry had joined the Army instead of the Navy?"

A panorama of historical possibilities opens up. Each student can now imagine a new history for Japan or the United States. Perhaps President Fillmore would have sent another man who would have done the same things Perry did. But if not, Japan might still be feudal today. Or Japan might have become part of the Soviet Union. Since there would have been no Pearl Harbor attack, the United States might have stayed out of World War II. On the contrary, we might have entered the war sooner because there would have been no worries about what Japan was going to do. And so on.

This is the inquiry, or problem-solving, method of teaching. Instead of presenting the student with the facts and nothing but the facts (Perry visited Japan. A treaty resulted), or with conventional interpretations (Perry brought Japan into the modern world), it poses a problem for the student and lets him do his own thinking.

At least three advantages are inherent in this method. First, the student has more fun participating in an imagination game than passively soaking up facts from the teacher or the textbook. Fun makes learning more effective.

Second, he has a chance to compare real events with hypothetical events. The comparison improves his grasp of the real events and makes their implications clearer to him.

Third, he has practice in productive thinking. Since the student will not always be in school, where someone knows all the right answers or seems to know them, he should learn to produce answers for himself as early in his career as possible.

## Evaluation

In the solution of practical problems as well as in creative work, it is not enough to have a variety of good ideas or to see a number of possible actions that can be taken. The thinker must usually choose one or a few alternatives and reject the others. In order to choose well, he must know which possibilities are most correct, suitable, adequate, or desirable. He must, in other words, exercise his judgment. In the Structure of Intellect theory, the judgmental process is called evaluation.

Judgment, or evaluation, occurs in all human activities. It occurs when you amuse yourself by trying to answer a question like "What's wrong with this picture?" A student practices evaluation when he decides whether a statement is logical, whether a sentence is complete, or which of two words sounds better in a sentence.

The businessman dictating a letter judges whether it is best to end it with *sincerely, cordially,* or *respectfully.* The voter evaluates the candidates before casting a vote.

*Vote for one.*

A husband needs all his powers of evaluation to respond to feminine queries like "Which looks better on me?"

The engineer selects the best material for the bridge. The menu planner has the good sense to avoid combinations like ravioli, fried rice, and baked potatoes. The employee knows whether to call his new boss Alf, A. E., or Mister Neuman.

Some evaluative decisions are made under pressure. A husband calls to his wife, "The smoke's getting thicker! What shall we save now?" The startled driver wonders, "Shall I try to squeeze between those trucks or run off the road?" The defense lawyer asks his client, "Do you want to plead guilty and throw yourself on the mercy of the court, or not guilty by reason of insanity?"

Except in a very rudimentary form, human judgment is not something we are born with. The ability to make correct decisions about problems of living and work must be learned.

Evaluation can be taught in school, if time is devoted to the exercise of judgment, and if the teacher encourages students to reach their own decisions. Naturally, there should be little ultimate disagreement on the facts of history, the laws of physics, or the rules of mathematics or grammar. But during the process of learning there should be plenty of room for considering alternatives, expressing preferences, and arriving at conclusions independently. The student cannot become a thinker by swallowing the facts whole. He can become a thinker only by working with information.

In the hypothetical problem in which Matthew Perry becomes an army officer, the students imagine many possible historical outcomes. Not all of the imagined outcomes are plausible. Some are more desirable than others. Each student's idea is evaluated by members of the class, who give their reasons for rating it high or low in plausibility or desirability. The teacher helps the class to see the implications that may be missed.

In the end, the students not only know what happened in history, but they care about it; and they have learned something about using independent judgment. Such interest and judgmental skills will be indispensable in the later exercise of adult responsibility, when there will be no teacher to give the facts or to act as referee and guide.

*Poet and Parent*

Household reality training often puts an exclusive emphasis on learning the rules and remembering the facts. It effectively discourages creative or inventive thinking and the practice of judgment.

The world is round, and children are not supposed to think it is flat, but how many parents listen all the way through the terrifying tale of the ships that fell off the edge before presenting the conventional view? Good manners are a subject of daily instruction in many families, but how many parents have asked a child to explain, from his own understanding, why people try to treat each other with consideration? Not many. The consequent short-circuiting of productive and evaluative thinking by the immediate parental presentation of facts and rules is not good preparation for later learning through active inquiry at school. Prominent among the essentials of human thinking is the ability to distinguish one thing from another: A is not B, dog is not cat, real is not imaginary. Mastery of what is real requires a corresponding mastery of what is not real. The first thing one must know in order to understand a dream is that it *was* a dream. Without comprehending the fact of its unreality, one cannot understand anything else about it. The more you know about what isn't, the more you know about what is.

How can the parent help the child to master both the real and the imaginary? An important step is to allow the child full expression of the fantasy before introducing the reality with which it should be compared. In interpersonal communication, full expression depends partly on a show of appreciation by the listener. The appreciation should be genuine, and it should be shown. After the parent has listened, with enjoyment, all the way through the child's version of what is, he can offer his own version — presumed to be a more realistic one.

The games in this book are directed visual fantasies that a parent can read to a child or a group of children. Playing them constitutes a kind of reality training that does not discourage imagination. While reading the games to the child, the parent can learn more about how to allow and reward the expression of imagination. The child can learn that there are times for fantasy and times for realism, and that each is good in its own time.

*My Son, the Spectator*

When a child is exposed to the products of other people's imagination he is not necessarily taught to use his own imagination. The average high school graduate is reported to have completed 10,800 hours of schooling and to have watched 15,000 hours of television. Only sleeping has taken up more of his time. A great many of those television hours, especially during the preschool and early school years, have been spent watching animated cartoons and live action fantasies.

Television and comic books can hardly be expected to cultivate a child's imagination, because the fantasy is already completely formed, on the screen or on the page. Nothing is left for the child to do but absorb it. If the child carries the ready-made commercial fantasy over into his own play, his use of it may be original or imitative. If he reads *Alice in Wonderland* or *The Hobbit*, most of the imagining will already have been done by Lewis Carroll or Tolkien, but the child must visualize the scenes, which is a great improvement over pure spectatorship. Imagination games require even more creative participation.

*A New Track*

The Freudian theory of mental defenses explains why imagination may not always be available for use. Defense mechanisms are mental tricks that protect us from anxiety. These tricks are learned and used unwittingly. When they are used, ideas that might make us uncomfortable are replaced by other, more comfortable ideas. Thoughts of next Sunday in the country help us to forget that this Friday we must visit the dentist. What we did to get a certain job is easily recalled, but not what we did to lose it. The lovely evening with the Joneses is brighter in memory than the awful night the Smiths left before dessert. In each case, the defense mechanism selects the pleasant thought for us, without letting us know that an unpleasant alternative also exists. In action, it may be compared to an automatic switch for a metaphorical train. Just before a dark and spooky tunnel comes into view around the bend, a switch is thrown, and the train (of thought) is deflected down a new track where sunnier prospects lie. The passenger does not realize what has happened. For most people, it works very well, most of the time.

Defense mechanisms are part of the normal mental equipment, but many people maintain more of this equipment than they need. There is a tendency never to throw any of it away. A clutter of old defenses can constrict or impoverish mental activity, protecting us not just from uncomfortable thoughts but from thoughts that are merely unfamiliar. If nightmares can be frightening, perhaps it isn't safe to imagine anything. One purpose of imagination games is to reclaim mental territory, to run the train of thought down many mental tracks and get rid of old defensive switches. By visualizing unfamiliar events, which may at first be scary, the player learns that the domain of imagination is larger and safer than he thought.

*Visualization*

Imagination games provide practice in visualizing. During the eighteenth and nineteenth centuries, visual and nonvisual mental imagery was a subject of much interest to philosophers and psychologists. When the conceptions of the mentalists were swept away by the tide of behaviorism in the early twentieth century, questions of inner experience were left largely to the psychoanalysts. Neither the Freudians nor even the Jungians were concerned with the study or cultivation of mental imagery as an ability. They wanted images all right, usually dream images, but they wanted them as symbols of complex motivations, which they then interpreted to their patients.

Along with other mental abilities, visualization is being studied by some modern psychologists. Several different kinds of visualization are now recognized as factors of intellect that contribute to creative effort in many fields involving the understanding and manipulation of form and space. Visualization enters into such disparate activities as painting, sculpture, choreography, architecture, astronautics, engineering, and photography. It is also helpful in playing baseball, moving furniture, and driving a car. An extreme example of the use of visualization may be found in the mental life of the formerly sighted person who is now blind; but most of us rely on visualization and other kinds of mental imagery more than we realize.

It comes as a surprise to many people that the ability to visualize is not uniformly distributed throughout the populace. Some people report having dreams or waking mental images that are sharp, bright, enduring, and full of color. Other people's visualizations are limited to gray tones, with occasional impressions of color. Still others have only hazy or intermittent impressions. A few swear that they cannot visualize anything at all.

These individual differences in the ability to visualize may occasionally be noted in playing imagination games, but they do not constitute an obstacle, and they can generally be ignored. Despite the wide range of differences, visualization is a common human ability. Furthermore, it is very unusual for anyone, especially a child, to say that he cannot *imagine* anything. A person who can *imagine*, or *pretend*, can play imagination games. In a group of children playing the games, we may be sure that some are experiencing more vivid, exact, and constant images than others. But each is imagining in his own way. That is all that is necessary.

*The Wise Child*

Part of the so-called cultural revolution among the younger members of our society is an increased valuation of nonverbal inner experience, involving mental images. Various chemical compounds have been used to "expand" the mind. One of the more powerful chemical agents, LSD, seems in some cases to expand the mind rather as a firecracker expands a tin can, leaving it battered and full of holes.

As a corrective to this unfortunate playing with fire in the brain, some serious persons are evincing a renewed interest in purely mental methods of expanding consciousness. The purposive use of imagery, for example, is an ancient means of mental development. Modern psychological conceptions can make it useful in the twenty-first century.

People can learn to be intuitive and expressive, flexible and perceptive, and they can do it without giving up reason, communication, purpose, or emotional control. They can learn to distinguish  the inner from the outer world without destroying either.

It helps to start this learning as a child.

# HOW
# TO
# PUT
# MOTHER
# ON
# THE
# CEILING

It takes at least two people to play imagination games. One person is the child. The other may be a parent, a teacher, an adult friend, or a teenager. The older player holds the book and reads it to the younger.

Each game has a short introduction that gives some idea of what the game is about and establishes a reference point in reality for that game. Remember that while these are imagination games, they are also a kind of reality training.

The name of each game is given at the beginning of the game and requested from the child at the end. If the child does not remember the name, you can remind him. The name serves as a signal that the game is ending and that the rules of reality are in effect again, until the next game begins.

At the end of each period of play, it is a good idea to play either "Here" or "Touch," games whose purpose is to bring the child's attention back to reality.

In general, earlier games are easier than later games. For best results, play the games in the order given in the book. Of course, it is always all right to go back and repeat an earlier game, but do not jump ahead to games you think might be more interesting. Work your way up to them. That way, the child should get the most out of each game.

Allow the child to repeat any game or part of a game whenever he wishes.

At the end of each game you will find open-ended questions: "What would you like to do now? / What now? / What now?" These are important. They allow the child to complete the game in a way that satisfies him. If the child wishes to make up an imagination game of his own, encourage him to go on with it as long as time permits and fun continues. Such spontaneous flights of fancy should take precedence over the games as written. You can always come back to the book, but the child's creative act of imagination must be caught when it happens.

*The Right Time and Place*

The sure test of the right time and place is enjoyment. Whenever both players enjoy the game, the time and place are right. Two conditions will help make it happen.

The first condition is the *absence of distraction.* It takes concentration to put Mother on the ceiling — at first, anyway. The television set should be turned off. Household pets and children who do not want to play should not be chasing each other around the players.

An even more important condition is the *desire to play.* Completely voluntary participation may not always be necessary for reading stories or playing checkers, but it is indispensable for imagination games. A nagged parent, for example, is likely to try to hurry the child through the game — which will spoil the game altogether. If either player is at all reluctant, put off playing until later.

Before beginning, it is a good idea to set a time limit or agree on how many games are to be played.

*The Child Sets the Pace*

The games must be read in a special way. Stop after every idea. The end of an idea is marked by a slant (/) or a paragraph. Do not read the next idea until the child signals that he wants to go on. Different children will have different ways of signaling. Some will say "Okay" or "Um-hm." Some will nod their heads. Some will look up expectantly. It does not matter how it is done, just so the message gets across. Some children may not signal at all. Then you will have to ask questions and work out a signal that is satisfactory to both players.

It is important not to confuse the child by going ahead with the next idea before he has completed the current one. Some children will play fast, others will play slow. Periods of silence are not a waste of time. The child is doing something. If you get bored waiting, make some images of your own.

Some children will play without saying much. Others will want to tell you just what is going on in their imaginations. Either way is all right. In fact, practically anything the child enjoys is all right. When you say, "Let us imagine a boy," the child may proceed to tell you a story about a boy. Let him tell it. While you are listening to the story, you can amuse yourself by making some images of it. When the story is finished, you can get back to the book.

In addition to the open-ended questions that are at the end of each game, other direct questions will be found here and there, in the short introductions and in the games themselves. The child may be asked, for example, what color he has made the girl's hat, or which teacher he is imagining. These direct questions may be answered as briefly or as fully as the child wishes. Even the silent player will usually answer them, and his answers will help you to know more about his feelings and his imagery.

When the games are played with groups of children, it will be helpful to work out a common signal for the completion of an idea, such as raising the hand. If there is much difference in speed among the players, it may be a good idea to assign them to fast and slow groups that can be conducted at different times or by different leaders.

When children in a group answer the direct questions in the games, you may not be able to take account of all their different answers, but the children will enjoy hearing and commenting on each other's ideas. Be sure to allow plenty of time for this exchange of ideas in the group. When you come to the open-ended questions at the end of each game, you can either select appealing images from those offered by the members of the group, or you can allow a period of individualized silent imagining.

*Step-by-Step Achievement*

In general, the book and the individual games progress from easy to difficult. This is in accordance with the principle of step-by-step achievement. When any difficulties are encountered, they can usually be overcome by applying the same principle.

For example, the first game, "Boys and Girls," starts in the realm of possibility and progresses to actions that can occur only in a world of fantasy. First a boy is standing on the floor, next he is walking, then he is jumping. Finally he floats up to the ceiling.

Some players who are just starting out may have difficulty disregarding the rules of the real world, such as the law of gravity. A boy may seem too heavy to float up to the ceiling, even in imagination. If the child believes that his imagination must follow the rules of reality, he will say something like, "The boy is too heavy," or "He can't float up there."

Point out to the child that he does not have to follow the rules of reality when he is imagining things. Say, "If that were a real boy, he wouldn't be able to float to the ceiling, would he? But he is a pretend boy, an imaginary boy. In your imagination, he can float up to the ceiling, if you want him to."

A clear statement of the lack of constraints in the world of fantasy may be all that is needed to overcome the difficulty. If it is not — if the child continues to say that the boy cannot do this or that — then it is time to resort to step-by-step achievement.

In using the principle of step-by-step achievement, we make the following assumption: *For every imaginary event that is difficult to imagine because it contradicts the rules of reality there is a lesser, similar event that will present little or no difficulty.* If reality cannot be contradicted all at once, it can be contradicted by degrees.

If, for example, the child cannot get an imaginary chair to float up to the ceiling, perhaps be can get a balloon or a feather to do it. Once the first step is accomplished, succeeding steps usually follow easily. A balloon, a feather, a pencil, a ball, a book, a pillow, a suitcase, a chair, a bed, a car, a boat, a battleship, a mountain, a planet, the sun — all things may be accomplished. The trick is to find the first, easy step.

Some children, without asking for help, solve such problems by employing realistic aids and devices. When you say, "Change the color of the girl's hat," the child, without saying a thing, may imagine that a salesperson walks up to the girl, removes her hat, and replaces it with a new hat of a different color. The ingenuity of this solution bespeaks a clever child, but the solution itself is undesirable. Our purpose is not to compromise between reality and imagination but to distinguish them clearly and separate them effectively.

Check on this point. Ask the child, "How did the hat change color?" If he answers, "It just changed," or "I changed it," all is probably well. If he admits using realistic aids, like paint or new hats, ask him to change the color without using anything, just by imagining that the hat is a different color. Once you have given him the idea, he may be able to carry it out immediately, with no trouble at all.

The blue hat that stubbornly refuses to become a red one can be changed into a red one step by step. Ask the child to have just one red button on the hat. Then two red buttons. Then a lot. When, finally, the hat is completely covered with red buttons, it will be a red hat, of a sort. By that time, the child will probably be able to take away all the buttons and have the hat be red without any buttons. One or two repetitions of this procedure ought to give the child complete control of the hat and its color.

In the floating-chair exercise, you may learn by questioning the child that he is raising the chair with a hydraulic jack, or with the help of balloons or birds tied to the chair. Your job is to show him that he does not need such aids. One way is to go through the balloon-feather-pencil-ball kind of sequence. Another way is to diminish the aids gradually. Have the balloons or birds grow smaller or fewer, until they are no longer needed.

The method is not important, so long as it helps the child to distinguish reality from imagination and discover that he is master of his imagination.

An imaginary activity that may give some players trouble is seeing at a distance. When you ask the child to imagine something going on in the yard at his school, he may say, "It's too far away. I can't see it." This problem can be handled step by step.

An easy visualization is to look at the room in which the game is being played, then close the eyes and see a mental image of it. If the child can do that, then ask him to remember or imagine how the next room looks. Then another familiar room that is farther away — perhaps your garage, or a neighbor's or relative's living room. After that, more and more distant places can be visualized, until the school yard — or the North Pole — is within easy reach. Do not be concerned about the vividness of the images. The child only has to say that he imagines or remembers how a place looks. The brightness, completeness, or constancy of the mental image is unimportant.

If, after all methods have been tried, the child says he simply cannot accomplish the required task, ask him, "How do you feel about that?" Allow him to tell you how he feels, whether much or little, and to give you any reasons he has for his failure. Accept his reasons or excuses, whatever they are and however illogical they may seem, without criticism. Ask him what he wishes to do about it.

If he is eager to go on with the game, then go on. If he wants to stop playing, then stop. But first try to interest him in playing "Here" and "Touch" for a few minutes, until he becomes cheerful. At the next opportunity, when both of you feel like playing imagination games again, begin play at the start of the game in which failure occurred. You may encounter no difficulty. If he still can't play that game, go back to a game he can play.

In group play, as with group instruction at school, it will not always be convenient to help individual players who report having difficulties. The group leader, like the teacher, will have to decide how much attention can be given to individual players. Difficulties should not be frequent in groups, however, because the fact that several other children are following the instructions successfully will make the games seem easier to each individual group member.

*Persistent Images*

During one game or another, the child may tell you that a particular image is "still there," when the instructions have called for its metamorphosis or disappearance. For example, when a crowd of children has been imagined in the school yard and you say, "Look at the school yard and see that the children are all gone," the answer may be, "They are still there."

This is apt to occur when the child has a particular liking for or interest in the persistent image. He may feel that it is beautiful, valuable, or hard to replace. We might theorize, for instance, that a lonely child would be disinclined to give up a crowd of imaginary children in the school yard. A child raised in poverty might hang on to images of toys, money, or food. And so on.

Whatever the particular image, the remedy for persistence is to create more images of the same kind, increase the supply, alleviate the scarcity, and thus reduce the demand. You can see that this is a sort of supply-and-demand economics of mental images. The child who finds that he can create as many of the desired images as he wants, whenever he wants, will not be upset at temporarily giving them up for something else.

The persistence of images where change or emptiness has been requested is counteracted, then, by the simple expedient of producing an oversupply of images. A typical solution of such a persistence problem might go as follows:

PARENT: Look at the school yard and see that there are no children there.

CHILD: I see some children.

PARENT: Have them go home. / Now look and see that there are no children in the school yard.

CHILD: There still are some. They are playing ball.

PARENT: Do you want them to stay?

CHILD: No. I am telling them to go home, but they stay anyway.

PARENT: Have some more children in the school yard, then.

CHILD: All right.

PARENT: Have more. Fill the school yard up with them.

CHILD: It's all full now.

PARENT: Squeeze some more children in.

CHILD: There's no room to play ball or anything.

PARENT:     Have one of the children go home.

CHILD:      *(Slightly worried)* All right.

PARENT:     Look all around the school yard for that child and
            see that that child is not there anymore.

CHILD:      The others are still there.

PARENT:     Yes, the others are still there. Now look around for
            the one you sent home.

CHILD:      *(Mild surprise)* He's gone. *(Satisfaction)* I sent him
            home.

PARENT:     Send some more of them home. / Look around
            the school yard and see that they are gone.

CHILD:      They're gone.

PARENT:     Send some more home.

CHILD:      It's almost empty now.

PARENT:     Can you send all the rest of them home?

CHILD:      Yes. They're all gone now.

PARENT:     Do you want to bring them back?

CHILD:      Yes.

PARENT:     Bring them all back. Pack them in tight. / Send
            them all home again. / Bring them back. / Have
            them disappear. / Have them be there again. /
            Send them all home.

CHILD:      I'm going to let them all stay home now. It's time
            for them to go to bed.

PARENT:     Is the school yard empty?

CHILD:      Yes. There is nobody there.

PARENT:     Not even one person?

CHILD:      No.

PARENT:     Is that all right?

CHILD:      Yes.

PARENT:     What do you want to do now?

CHILD:      Let's finish the game.

*What Does This Game Do?*

It would not be difficult to list the various meanings that the different games might have for children, or feelings that they might arouse. I could say, for example, that children sometimes worry about their parents' being hurt or getting lost, and that the game called "Parents" produces an oversupply of parental images and puts them through their paces until the child finally feels he has parental images to burn. This, in turn, could reduce any realistic concern he might feel about the safety or availability of his real parents.

No such list of psychological hypotheses or findings could guarantee, however, that any game would mean some particular thing to your individual child. Since it is your child you are interested in, and not some statistical trend among children, such theoretical speculations should be avoided while playing the games, lest they become an obstacle.

Suppose the child says he does not want to imagine Mother on the roof because she might fall off and get killed. Do not become an amateur psychoanalyst and start to wonder about his dependency feelings or his ambivalence. Do not yourself confuse reality with imagination by assuring him that you are not afraid to be on the roof. Just handle the problem step by step. Whom can he have on the roof, if not Mother? How near the edge? Is a fence needed for a little while?

When several dozen assorted images have fallen off the roof, some shattering to bits, others bouncing, laughing, waving flags, the child will see that the activity is under his control and that he can afford to put Mother or anybody on the roof. It is mastery that counts, not explanations.

*Parents' Imagination Games*

There is no rule against exercise of the parent's imagination. Even before you have gone all the way through the book, you may find yourself inspired to make up some games of your own, or to modify the games in the book. Except for the rule that the child should go through the games the first time in the order given, you should feel free to improvise. In all improvisations, it will help to remember the principle of step-by-step achievement.

Some minor modifications may be in order the first time through. You will notice, for example, that I have frequently used the word *house*. "Have Mother go outside of the *house*." "Move all the beds in the *house*." "Throw those houses away." And so on. More and more people in our society are living in apartments and other non-houses, especially in the city. If you live in a non-house, you should feel free to change house to whatever word seems natural. On the other hand, *house* is a nice short word that tends to stand for almost any kind of dwelling, and so you may not feel that it is necessary to change it, even if you do not live in a house.

In the game called "Home," you will find an explicit opportunity to improvise. Since I do not know what your home looks like, how many rooms it has, or what the furnishings and decorations are, I have provided a paragraph with some blanks for you to fill. If you are living on a boat, you can work out some nautical adaptations — "Put your Captain on the ceiling. / Have the binnacle in the bunk," and so on.

In the last game, "Touch," there are blanks for *real* objects.

Do not hesitate to make the games more enjoyable for your child by changing unfamiliar things to things that are familiar. In "Being Things," the child is asked to imagine that he is Mother, Father, Brother, Sister, Aunt, and Uncle. You may wish to omit all but actual relatives. On the other hand, it will probably be easy for the child to imagine himself an uncle, even if he has no uncle.

If the child has no father, you can avoid awkwardness the first time or two the term *Father is* used by changing it to *a father* or *someone's father*. If the child's father is never called anything but Daddy, Pop, or Ralph, you may wish to substitute the more familiar name.

If the child is puzzled by the word *steamroller,* you will have to describe how a steamroller looks and what it does. Play it by ear. The act of imagining is the important thing — not any particular word or image.

Often you will find alternate words provided in the text — *boy (girl), him (her)* — and you will have to decide which to use. The choice will sometimes be clear from what has just happened in the game, but when there is ambiguity it will usually be best to choose the same-sex word, so that boy players can imagine boys, and girl players can imagine girls. Examples of this will be found in "Manners" and "Baby." In "Manners," the whole game should be played using the same-sex word, even though *her* is usually omitted from the text. If the child wants to play "Manners" again, you can then use the opposite-sex word, for variety.

With mixed groups, Manners should be played twice, so as not to slight either sex. This procedure may elicit comments from the boys about the girls, and vice versa.

Now and then you will find a sequence like the following: "Have someone standing on the table. / Have him (her) jump off." If the child does not tell you who is standing on the table, you will not know which sex is correct. You can either ask, or use the conventional *him* until you are corrected by the child. When playing with groups, you will find it most practical in such cases to say "him or her."

In making up your own games, see that the rules of reality are broken as often as they are kept. Water should run uphill. Dogs should meow. Fish should fly. Outrageous flouting of the rules will help the child to distinguish reality from imagination.

Between your games, don't forget to touch down to reality. A good way is to talk realistically about some of the ideas in the game. "Here" and "Touch" will provide further contrast between what is real and what is not. Play them at the end.

Now that you have read through both of these introductory chapters, if there is anything that you are still puzzled about, don't worry. Your child will probably be able to explain it to you after a game or two.

# The
# Games

# Boys and Girls

*You can put your clothes on or take them off. You can take off a red jacket at the store and put on a green one. But can you change a red jacket into a green one? Or change a cat into a dog? It's easy — in your imagination.*

The name of this game is BOYS AND GIRLS.

Let us imagine that there is a boy standing in the corner of this room. / Let us give him a hat. / What color would you like the hat to be? / Let us give him a jacket. / What color jacket shall we give him? / Let us give him some trousers. / What color do you want his trousers to be? / Let him have some shoes. / What color will you let him have?

Now change the color of his hat. / What color did you change it to? / Change it again. / What color this time? / Look at his jacket. What color is it? / Change it to another color. / Change it again. / What color are his trousers now? / Change the color of his trousers. / Change them again. / What color are his shoes now? / Change them to another color. / Change them again. / What color are they now?

Have him stand on one foot and hold his other foot straight out in front of him. / Have him stand on the other foot. / Have him walk over to another corner of the room. / Have him go to another corner. / Have him sing a song. / Have him go to another corner.

Have him lie down and roll across the floor. / Have him run around on his hands and knees. / Have him stand on his hands. / Have him sing a song while he is standing on his hands. / Have him run around the room on his hands.

Have him stand on his feet. / Have him jump up into the air. / Have him jump up higher. / Have him jump up and touch the ceiling. / Have him sit in a chair. / Have the chair float up to the ceiling and stay there. / Have the boy sing something while he sits up there. / Have the chair come down. / Have the boy float up to the ceiling without the chair. / Have him float to a corner of the room up there. / Have him float to another corner. / Have him sing his favorite song.

Have him come down to the floor. / Have him say "Good-bye" and go out the door to visit a friend. / Look into one corner of the room and see that he is not in that corner. / Look into another corner and see that he is not there either. / Look into all the other corners, above and below, and find that he is not in any of them.

Put a girl in one corner of the room. / Give her a red hat. / Give her a blue sweater. / Give her a green skirt. / Give her brown shoes. / Now make her hat blue. / Make her sweater yellow. / Make her skirt purple. / Make her shoes black. / Change them to green. / Change them to yellow.

/ Change all her clothes to white. / Change them to purple. / Change them to green.

Have her be in another corner of the room. / Have her be in another corner. / Have her sing a song.

Have her float up to the ceiling. / Have her turn upside down and stand on the ceiling. / Have her walk all around the ceiling, looking for the boy who was there before. / Have her look in all the corners up there and find that be is not in any of them.

Bring the boy back and put him on the ceiling with the girl. / Have them standing on the ceiling playing ball. / Put another boy and another girl on the ceiling with them, and have all four playing ball. / Put some more boys and girls on the ceiling, and have them all playing ball. / Turn them all right side up, and put them on the roof . / Put them in the play yard at school. / Make twice as many of them, and have them all shouting.

Make a new crowd of boys and girls on the ceiling. / Put them on the roof. / Put them in the school yard. / Have all the children shouting and running around.

Look at the ceiling and see that there are no children there. / Put one boy there. / Put him in the school yard. / Put one girl on the ceiling. / Put her in the school yard.

Have no one on the ceiling. / Have it full of boys and girls. / Have it empty again. / Have no one on the roof. / Have it covered with boys and girls. / Have it empty again.

/ Have no one in the school yard. / Have it full of boys and girls. / Have it empty again.

Put one child in the school yard. / Is it a boy or a girl? / What color are his (her) clothes? / What would you like to do with him (her)? / All right, do it.

What is the name of the game we just played?

# Animals

*Have you ever seen a live elephant as small as a mouse?*
*Are there any real elephants that small, in India or Africa,*
*or at the zoo or the circus? I don't think so.*

This game is called ANIMALS.

We are going to start with one little mouse, and see what we
can do.

Let us imagine that there is a little mouse somewhere in the
room. Where would you like to put him? / All right, have

him sit up and wave to you. / Have him turn green. / Change his color again. / Change it again. / Have him stand on his hands. / Have him run over to the wall. / Have him run up the wall. / Have him sit upside down on the ceiling. / Turn him right side up and put him in a corner up there. / Put another mouse in another corner up there. / Put a mouse in each of the other two corners up there. / Put other mice in the four corners down below. / Are they all there? / Turn them all yellow. / Have them all say "Hello" at the same time. / Have them all say "How are you?" / Have them all promise to stay in their corners and watch the rest of the game.

Put a little dog right over there *(Pointing)*. / Have him bark. / Have him sit up and laugh. / Give him the name Felix. / Ask him his name and have him answer Felix. / Have him grow bigger. / Have him grow smaller. / Have him grow much smaller. / Have him grow so small that he is no bigger than a pea. / Have him turn into a cat no bigger than a pea. / Have the cat grow as big as a potato. / Have it grow as big as your head. / Have it grow into a big, fat blue cat. / Have it turn into a horse but stay the same size.

Are the yellow mice all in their places? Have them clap their hands because the cat turned into a little horse. / Have the little horse grow bigger. / Have him grow bigger still. / Have him grow very big. / Have him become little again. / Have him be as big as your head. / Have him be as big as your hand. / Have him be as big as your thumb.

Ask him his name and have him tell you George. / Change his name to Rudolph. / Ask him his name and have him tell you Rudolph. / Change his name to Harry. / Ask him his name and have him tell you Harry. / Take away his name. / Ask him his name and have him shake his head. / Pick a good name for him and give it to him. / Ask him his name and have him tell you that name.

Is he as big as your thumb? / Change him into an elephant but keep him the same size. / Have him grow as big as a pumpkin. / Have him grow as big as your bed. / Have him grow as big as you want him to be. / How big is he?

Have him shrink until he is as small as your thumb. / Have him shrink until he is no bigger than a pea. / Have him be no bigger than a pinhead. / Have him shrink until there is nothing left of him at all.

Look at the place where he was and see that he is not there. / Have the yellow mice clap their hands in admiration. / Put a new elephant there. / Make him as big as a police dog. / Make him as big as a cat. / Make him as big as a mouse. / Make him as big as a pea. / Have him shrink away to nothing.

Look where he was and see that there is nothing there. / Have the yellow mice cheer and wave their arms and legs. / Put a new elephant where the other one was. / Make him as big as you want to make him. / Make him as small as you want to make him. / Have him shrink away to nothing.

Look where he was and see that there is no elephant there. / Have the yellow mice write letters home to their friends to tell what wonderful things you do with elephants.

Put a new elephant there. / Change him to a dog. / Change the dog to a cat. / Change the cat to a mouse. /

Change the mouse to a pea. / Change the pea to nothing. / Look and see that there is no pea there.

Put a new pea there. / Have it not be there. / Have a dog there. / Have no dog there. / Have a cat there. / Have no cat there. / Have an elephant there. / Have no elephant there.

Have the yellow mice clap their hands. / Have them come to the place where the elephant was. / Have them grow smaller. / Have them grow smaller still. / Have no mice there. / Have some new mice there. / Make them blue. / Have no mice there.

Have one mouse there. / What color do you want it to be? / What do you want to do with it? / All right, do it.

What was the name of the game we just played?

# Mother

*Mother could climb up a ladder and touch the ceiling, couldn't she? I think so. But could she stand on the ceiling? I never heard of a mother doing that.*

This game is called MOTHER.

Let us imagine that Mother is standing right there (pointing). / Let's give Mother a hat. / What color hat will you give her? / What color dress will you give her? / What color shoes will you give her? / All right, change the color of her hat. / Change the color of her shoes. / Change the color of her dress.

Have her go to a different part of the room. / Have her go into another room. / Have her go outside the house. / Have her coming in the front door. / Have her cooking in the kitchen. / Have her setting the table. / Have her asleep in her bed. / Have her washing the dishes. / Have her making the bed. / Have her singing. / Have her talking on the telephone.

Have her standing on the roof. / Have her taking a bath in the bathroom. / Have her cooking dinner outdoors. / Have her sitting on top of a box. / Have her sitting on a ladder. / Have her sitting in a tree. / Have her cooking dinner up in a tree. / Have her taking a bath up in the tree. / Have her asleep in her bed up in the tree.

Have Mother at the store, buying things. / Have her buy something nice for you. / Have her come home and give it to you. / Have her walking through a forest. / Have her standing on top of a mountain. / Have her on a boat. / Have her swimming in a swimming pool. / Have her swimming in a lake. / Have her swimming in the ocean.

Have her riding a horse. / Have her riding a camel. / Have her riding an elephant. / Have her riding a tiger. / Have her riding a donkey. / Have her riding a rocking horse.

Have her riding in a car. / Have her riding a bicycle. / Have her riding a motorcycle. / Have her flying in a plane. / Have her riding in a spaceship to the moon. / Have her cooking dinner on the moon. / Have her making beds on the moon. / Have her reading you a story on the moon.

Have Mother walking through a jungle. / Have her riding across a desert. / Have her driving a dog sled through the snow. / Have her rounding up a herd of cattle. / Have her walking on the bottom of a lake, looking at the fish. / Have her walking on the bottom of the ocean. / Have her cooking dinner on the bottom of the ocean. / Have her making beds on the bottom of the ocean. / Have her doing the ironing on the bottom of the ocean. / Have her reading you a story on the bottom of the ocean.

Have Mother sitting in a chair at home, combing her hair. / Have her sweeping the floor. / Have her looking in her mirror. / Have her washing her face. / Have her sitting at dinner.

What would you like to have Mother do now? / All right, have her do that. / Have her do something else. / Have her do something else.

How does Mother feel now? / Have her feel happy. / Have her thank you for putting her in all those interesting places. / Is there anything else you would like to do with Mother? / All right, do it.

What was the name of the game we just played?

# Father

---

*I am sure Father has never ridden a rhinoceros. I suppose he could, if he didn't get scared — or if the rhinoceros didn't get scared of him.*

This game is called FATHER.

Let us put Father right there (pointing). / Now give him a hat. / What color will you give him? / What color suit will you give him? / What color shoes will you give him?

Change the color of his hat. / Change the color of his suit. / Change the color of his shoes.

Take away Father's hat. / Take away his shoes. / Have him dressed in a bathing suit. / Have him dressed in armor. / Have him dressed in blue. / Have him dressed in green. / Have him dressed in red. What would you like him to wear now? / All right, have him dressed in that.

Have Father go to a different part of the room. / Have him float up to the ceiling. / Have him come down again. / Have him go into another room. / Have him standing on the roof. / Have him sitting in a tree. / Have him taking a bath. / Have him asleep in his bed.

Have Father riding a horse. / Have him riding a camel. / Have him riding a tiger. / Have him riding an elephant. / Have him riding a giraffe. / Have him riding a rhinoceros. / Have the rhinoceros flying.

Have Father in the closet. / Have him rolled in the rug. / Have him sitting on the stove. / Have him under the bed. / Have him climbing up the side of the house. / Have him wearing your clothes. / Have him riding your wagon. / Have him driving a car. / Have him riding a motorcycle. / Have him flying a plane. / Have him piloting a spaceship to Mars. / Have him helping you with your schoolwork on Mars. / Have him helping you with your schoolwork at home in the kitchen.

Have Father sitting upside down on the ceiling. / Have him playing marbles upside down on the ceiling. / Have Mother playing marbles with him. / Have them playing marbles on the roof. / Have them playing marbles in the school yard.

Have Mother and Father walking down the street. / Have them riding on a train. / Have them on a bus. / Have them on television. / Have them in the funny papers. / Have them in the park. / Have them at the seashore. / Have them in the kitchen.

Have Father sitting at the table for dinner. / Have him standing on the table. / Have him sitting under the table.

Have him up in that corner over there *(pointing)*. / Have him in another corner up there. / Have him in another corner. / In another corner.

What would you like to do with Father now? / All right, do it. / Is there anything else you would like to do with Father? / All right.

What was the name of the game we just played?

# **Home**

---

*We get used to the way things look, especially at home. We don't expect to see them changed. If we changed everything around in our house, do you think we could get used to it again? I suppose we could, after a while.*

This game is called HOME.

Do you know just how Home looks? / Do you know how all the rooms look? / Do you know where all the things are in all the rooms? / Let us play a game of changing everything around.

Let us take the stove out of the kitchen and put it in some other room. / What room would you like to put it in? / All right, now take the kitchen sink and put it with the stove. / How do they look together there? / Take something else out of the kitchen and put it with the stove and sink. / Take all the things that are left in the kitchen and pile them on the ceiling of the kitchen. / Turn the kitchen floor into glass. / Have some fish swimming under the floor. / Is there anything else you would like to do to the kitchen? / All right, do it.

Now change the bathroom all around. First, make it about twice as big. / Put the bathtub outside the window. / Have the toilet where the bathtub was. / Have the washbasin on the ceiling. / Have the medicine cabinet in the floor. / Have the toilet in the bathtub. / Have the door in the ceiling. / Is there anything else you would like to do to the bathroom? / All right, do it.

Now move all the beds in the house. Where would you like to put your bed? / Where would you like to put Mother's bed? / Are there any other beds you would like to move? / All right.

*(The following may be used for the remaining rooms, and varied at the discretion of the reader.)*

Now change the..........room around. Put the..........on the ceiling. / Have the ..........hanging on the wall. / Have the..........hanging on another wall. / Throw the.......... out the window. / Put the..........into another room. / Put the..........into the ground under the house. / Hide the..........in the.......... / Roll the.......... up in the.......... / Is there anything else you would like to change? / All right.

Now, let's look at the house from the outside. / How does it look? / Make the house taller and thinner. / Make it a little shorter and fatter. / Move it a little way from you. / Bring it a little closer to you. / Change the color of the house. / Put another house exactly like it right beside it. / Change the color of the houses again. / Change it again.

Turn the houses upside down. / Have trees grow up out of the bottoms of them. / Turn the houses into glass. / Turn them right side up. / Put them on another street. / Put them in another country. / Have them on top of a mountain. / Have them in a desert. / Have your friends riding camels all around them. / Have the houses floating on a lake. / Have your friends paddling canoes all around them.

Throw those houses away. / Have two new ones made of green bananas. / Turn the bananas blue. / Turn them yellow. / Turn them into feathers. / Turn them red. / Have all the feathers blow away. / Have no houses at all.

Have two new houses made of flowers. / Throw the flowers away. / Have no houses at all. / Have two houses made of sticks. / Throw the sticks away. / Have no houses. / Have two houses made of birds' nests. / Throw the birds' nests away. / Have no houses.

Have a big desert with no houses in it. / Look all around and see that there are no houses. / Have a big mountain with no houses on it. / Look all over it and see that there are no houses. / Have a large forest with no houses in it. / Look all through it and see that there are no houses in it.

Have a street with no houses on it. / Look up and down it and see that there are no houses. / Have lots of houses on it. / Have no houses on it. / Have one house on it.

Make the house bigger. / Make it smaller. / Make it any size you want it to be. / Is there anything else you would like to do with that house? / All right, do it.

What was the name of the game we just played?

# Jumbly

*I think it would be very hard for anybody to get along without his head. I don't think he could do it. I'm sure he couldn't. How would he know where to put his hat or his glasses? How would he blow his nose?*

This game is called JUMBLY.

Let us imagine that we take you apart and put you back together again.

Take off one of your feet and put it on the other side of the room. / Take off the other foot and put it beside the first foot. / Take off one leg and put it on the first foot. / Take off the other leg and put it on the other foot. / Take off your middle and put it on the legs. / Take off your chest and put it on the middle. / Take off your arms and shoulders and put them on the chest. / Have your hands on the ends of your arms. / Put your neck on top of the shoulders. / Put your head over there on the top of the neck.

Make a new body for yourself over here. / How does that other body look over there?

Take the feet off this new body and put them over there on the other side of the room. / Put the legs over there, too. / Put the middle over there. / Put the chest and shoulders and arms and hands over there. / Put the neck and head over there. / Make a new body for yourself over here.

How do those two bodies look over there?

Would you like to play Jumbly with them? / All right.

Switch the heads around. Take the head off the first body and put it on the second, and take the head off the second body and put it on the first. / Switch the necks. / Switch the shoulders and arms and hands. / Switch the chests. / Switch the middles. / Switch the legs. / Switch the feet.

How do they look now? / Would you like to jumble them even more? / All right.

Put the heads where the feet belong and put the feet where the heads belong. Do it with both bodies. / Have the legs where the arms belong and have the arms where the legs belong. / Have the necks where the stomachs belong and have the stomachs where the necks belong. / How do those bodies look now? / Pretty jumbly? / All right, throw them away and put two new bodies there. / Have them look ordinary.

Have the legs growing out of the tops of the heads. / Have the hands growing out of the feet. / Have the arms growing out of the hands. / Have the stomachs on top of the arms. / Have extra heads on top of the stomachs. / How do those bodies look now? / Very jumbly? / All right. Throw them away. / Put two new ones there.

Give the new bodies your name. / Ask them their names and have them tell you. / Now change their names to something else. / Ask them their names and have them tell you. / What would you like to change their names to now? / All right, change them to that. / Ask them their names and have them tell you.

Have them grow smaller. / Have them grow bigger. / Have them grow thinner. / Have them grow fatter. / Have them grow smaller. / Have them grow much smaller. / Have them shrink away to nothing. / Put two new ones there. / Switch their heads. / Have them turn to each other and say "Thank you."

What would you like to do with them now? / All right, do it.

What was the name of the game we just played?

# School

*What would happen at school if you were the teacher? What would happen if parents went to school? Suppose monkeys went to school. Do you think they would learn to read and write? Would they do what they were told?*

This game is called SCHOOL.

Let us imagine your schoolroom. / Let us have it empty. / No one in the seats. / No one at the teacher's desk. / No one at the blackboard. / Look all around the schoolroom and see that there is no one there.

Now, you be at the front of the room, teaching all the empty chairs. / Have books and pencils and papers at every place. / Have the pencils writing on the paper. / Have the pages of the books turning. / Have pieces of chalk writing on the blackboard. / Have the pieces of paper come up to the front of the room, to be graded. / Give some good marks and some bad marks. / Send them back to their places. / Tell all the empty places that school is out. / Have the books and pencils and papers rush out of the room.

Have a schoolroom full of children. / You be teaching them. / Have one boy put up his hand and ask to leave the room. / Let him go. / Have the others write a spelling lesson on their papers. / Have them add some numbers. / Send some of them to the blackboard to draw pictures. / Have the others bring their papers to you to be graded. / Give some good marks and some bad marks. / Tell the children that school is out. / Have them pick up their books and papers and pencils and walk out the door.

Have a schoolroom with big people sitting in all the chairs. / You be teaching them. / Have one of them stand up and spell a word. / Have another go to the blackboard and add some numbers. / Have another ask to leave the room. / Let him (her) go. / Have the other big people write on their papers about what they did during their vacations. / Have them bring the papers to you to be graded. / Give some good marks and some bad marks. / Tell the big people school is out. / Have them run out the door.

Have a schoolroom full of teachers. / You be teaching them. / What would you like to have one of them do? / All right. / What would you like to have another do? / All right. / (Continue asking the child what he would like to have the teachers do and have himself do in the scene, until he runs out of ideas.)

Have another schoolroom with no one in it. / You be the teacher. / Have the room full of monkeys, all jumping up and down. / Send them to the principal, to be scolded. / Have the room full of seals, all flapping their flippers. / Keep them in after school, as punishment. / Have the room full of lions, all roaring. / Send them to the blackboard to write, "I will not roar in school."

Have another schoolroom. / Have it full of children. / You be one of the children./ Have a teacher at the front of the room./ Have the teacher walk up the wall and sit in a chair on the ceiling. / Have the teacher playing the trumpet up there. / Have the teacher skating on the ceiling. / Have the teacher fly out the window. / Have the children fly out after her (him). / Look all around the schoolroom and see that it is empty.

What would you like to do with the schoolroom now? / All right. / What else? / All right.

What was the name of the game we just played?

# Parents

———————

*Parents need a lot of attention, don't they? — even one or two parents. Suppose you had a lot of parents. How would you keep track of them all?*

This game is called PARENTS.

Let us have Father right over there *(pointing.)* / Let us have Mother over there with him. / Ask them who they are, and have them say "Mother" and "Father." / Ask them who they are again, and have them say "Parents." / Have two of each. Two Mothers and two Fathers. / Have the two

Mothers just alike. / Have the two Fathers just alike. / Ask them all who they are and have them say "Parents."

Have the parents grow smaller. / Have them all turn green. / Have them grow smaller still. / Have them turn blue. / Have them grow bigger. / Have them turn red. / Have them grow bigger still. / Have them turn yellow. / Have them shrink until they are no bigger than pumpkins. / Have them turn orange. / Have them turn any color you like.

Put the little parents up in that corner *(pointing)*. / Put them all around in all the corners of the room, one corner after another. / Put them up on the roof. / Have them in a tree. / Have them on top of the tallest building in the world. / Have them down in the deepest mine in the world. / Have them on top of the tallest mountain in the world. / Have them at the bottom of the deepest ocean. / Have them in the school yard.

Have the little parents walking down the street. / Have a big dog run up and bark at them. / Have him growl at them. / Have the parents grow up bigger than the dog. /

Have the dog run away. / Have the parents grow little again. / Have the dog come back. / Have the parents grow big. / Have the dog run away. / Have the parents grow little.

Have a dragon come up and breathe fire at the little parents. / Have the parents grow big and breathe fire back at the dragon. / Have the dragon put his tail between his legs and yelp and run away, scattering sparks as he runs.

Have the parents grow little again. / Have them walking down the middle of the street. / Have them lie down in the street. / Have them become as flat as pancakes in the middle of the street. / Have them jump up and run around the street, still as flat as pancakes. / Have a steamroller standing in the middle of the street. / Have the pancake parents run and jump under the roller of the steamroller. / Have them fit nicely under there because they are so flat. / Have them feeling comfortable under there. / Have them grow big and upset the steamroller. / Have the parents run around laughing at the steamroller. / Have the steamroller burst into tears.

Have the four parents standing in the middle of the street. / Double the number, so that there are eight parents standing in the street. / Have the eight parents standing on a mountain. / Have them flying through the air. / Have them walking on the bottom of the ocean.

Have them swimming in the ocean. / Have a shark swim up and eat two of the eight parents. / Have the shark swim away. / Make two new parents there, to take the places of the ones that were eaten up. / Have another shark come up and eat two more of the parents. / Have the shark swim away. / Make two new parents to take the places of those that were eaten by the second shark.

Have another shark swim up to the parents. / Have him open his mouth to eat all the parents. / Have the parents grow much bigger. / Have them catch the shark and eat him all up. / Have them all say, "Mmm. That was good!"

Have the eight parents standing in the school yard. / Have four of them shrink until they are no bigger than pumpkins. / Have the same four be no bigger than peas. / Have the same four shrink away to nothing. / Have two more shrink away to nothing.

Have the two parents who are left turn blue. / Have them on the roof. / Have them in this room. / Make them any color you like. / Have them be little. / Put them in all the corners of the room, one corner after another. / Have them shrink away to nothing.

Have two new parents right there (pointing). / Have no parents there. / Have two parents there. / Have them wink at you. / What would you like to do with them now? / All right, do it.

What was the name of the game we just played?

# Party

---

*Sometimes other children get together and don't let you in. They might even have a party and not invite you. Would you feel unhappy? I would. But it happens to everybody sometimes.*

This game is called PARTY.

Let us imagine that there is a big party of boys and girls in the school yard. / Would you like to be at the party with them? / All right, be there with them.

Have all the children singing songs. / Are you singing too? / Have all the children playing with a big ball. / Have them sitting at a big table. / Have them eating good things. /

Have them standing on the table. / Have them pick up the table and carry it around the school yard. / Have them take it to a secret place and hide it. / Have them all go home. / Have the school yard empty.

Have one of your friends give a party. / Have the children you know go to the party. / You go to the party, too. / Have the party be over. / Have everyone go home.

Have the same friend give another party but not ask you to come. / Have all the children go to the party without you. / Go and stand outside the door of the house and ask them to let you in. / Have them let you in. / Have the party be a lot of fun. / Have the party be over. / Have everyone go home.

Have the same friend give another party and tell you that you can't come. / Go and stand outside the door of the house and ask to come in. / Have them tell you that you can't come in. / Shout at them that you want to come in. / Have them say "No." / Tell them you will blow the door down if they don't let you in. / Have them put their hands over their ears.

Take a deep breath and blow on the door of the house. / Have it fall in with a crash. / Go right into the house and join the party. / Have carpenters come and put the door back up. / Have everyone say you are a wonderfully strong blower. / Have the party be a lot of fun. / Have everyone go home.

Now you give a party, and invite everyone except the friend who kept you out. / Have all the others come. / Have your friend come and stand outside the door and ask to be let in. / Tell him (her) to stay out. / Have him (her) take a deep breath and blow the door down. / Have him (her) come in and join the party. / Have the party be a lot of fun. / Have everyone except your friend go home.

Give your friend a spanking for blowing down the door. / Have your friend crying. / Make your friend put the door back up. / Have your friend ask if he (she) may blow down the door again. / Let him (her) blow down the door once more. / Have him (her) put it back up again. / Shake hands with him (her). / Have your friend go home.

Give a party and invite everyone in the whole world. / Have them all come. / Have the party be a lot of fun. / Have the party be over. / Have them all go home.

Give a party and invite nobody. / Have nobody come. / Have the party be a lot of fun. / Have the whole world come. / Have the party be a lot of fun. / Have everyone go home.

Give a party and invite nobody. / Have nobody come. / Have the party be fun. / Even though nobody came to the party, have the whole world go home from the party.

Give a party and invite another you. / Have you come. / Have you go home. / Have a lot of yous come to the party. / Have them all go home. / Wave goodbye to them from the door.

What kind of a party would you like to give now? / All right, give it.

What was the name of the game we just played?

# Helping

*Sometimes you do things to help Mother and Father, but they don't like what you do. It's hard not to make mistakes. And it's hard to find things that really help. Does anyone ask you to help by keeping your room neat, or by being a good boy (girl)? Do you do it? Is it fun?*

This game is called HELPING.

Let us imagine that you are in the kitchen, helping Mother. / Wash the dishes. / Cook something. / Scrub the floor. /

Set the table. / Break something. / Pick it up and put it back together again. / Have it be as good as new.

Wash all the windows in the house. / Break one. / Go to the store and buy a new piece of glass for the window. / Put the new glass in the window.

Have your toys and possessions all around the house, making it untidy. / Have Mother and Father trip and fall over your things. / Have guests come and say, "What a messy house!" / Have Mother and Father feeling sad because the house is messy. / Have them go out for a walk. / Pick up your possessions and put them away. / Have new guests come and say, "What a neat and orderly house!"/ Have Mother and Father come home and be happy because the house is so neat.

Bring home a good report card from school and show it to Mother and Father. / Have them happy. / Bring home a bad report card and show it to them. / Have them sad. / Bring home a good report card. / Have them laughing.

Have Mother and Father catch the measles. / Take care of them while they are sick. / Make them stay in bed. / Read to them. / Cook for them. / Take them to the bathroom. / Take their temperatures. / Call the doctor. / Give Mother and Father lots and lots of medicine. / How does it taste to them? / Have them be well again. / Have them thank you for taking care of them.

Go out and get a job. / Come home from work and give Father a lot of money. / Give Mother some big packages of things to eat. / Buy some new clothes for yourself. / What kind will you buy? / Buy a new car for yourself. / Buy a new car for Mother and Father. / Buy another and keep it in your room.

Have the wind blow the roof of the house off. / Go up there and put a new roof on. / Have water leak into the house. / Get a bucket and carry the water out of the house. / Have some mosquitoes in the house. / Go around with a swatter and swat them. / Have Mother and Father thank you.

Ask Mother and Father to give you some more work to do around the house. / Have them say there is no work for you. / Make them stay indoors until they give you some work to do. / Have them thank you for doing the work.

Ask them for some more work. / Have them tell you that they will do everything themselves. / Get a long rope and tie them in their chairs. / Give them nothing to eat but bread and water. / Tell them to give you some more work. / Have them give you some. / Have them thank you for doing the work.

Have Mother and Father come to you and ask you what they can do to help you around the house. / Tell them there is nothing for them to do. / Tell them that you have a job and will buy everything for everybody. / Tell them that you will do all the cooking and cleaning. / Have them burst into tears because there is nothing for them to do. / Tell them they can help you by keeping their rooms neat. / Tell them they can help you by being good parents and not fighting or being rude. / Tell them they can help you by washing their faces and hands before meals and after meals without being told each time. / Have them thank you for letting them help you by doing these things.

What would you like to let them do now? / All right. / Anything else? / All right.

What was the name of the game we just played?

# Theater

*In the theater, the person on the stage does things, and the people in the audience watch. The person on the stage is called the performer. The performer hopes the audience will clap their hands or even cheer. If they don't even smile, the performer feels unhappy.*

This game is called THEATER.

Let us imagine that we have a theater. / Make it a big theater, with lots of seats. / Have a red curtain hanging at the front of the stage. / Turn the curtain green. / Have a lot of people in the seats, looking at the curtain. / You be one of the people sitting in the seats.

Have the curtain go up. / Have a girl walk out to the center of the stage. / Have the people in the audience clap. / Have the girl sing a song. / Have the audience clap again. / Have the girl leave the stage.

Have a man walk out and recite poetry. / Have the audience all nod their heads. / Have the man leave the stage.

Have a boy walk out and sing and recite. / Have the people clap. / Have a girl walk out and sing and recite. / Have the people clap again. / Have the boy and girl leave the stage.

Be up on the stage, looking out at the audience. / See all the bright lights shining toward you. / Say "Gobble-gobble-gobble," to the audience. / Have them clap. / Sing a song to them. / Have them cheer. / Have them go on clapping for a long time. / Do you like the way their clapping sounds?

Have them quiet again. / Be telling them a long story. / Have them listening very carefully. / Have them enjoying the story. / Have them hoping they can remember it, to tell their friends when they get home.

Be one of the people who are sitting in the audience. / See yourself up on the stage. / Hear yourself telling the story. / Lean over to the person who is sitting next to you in the audience and whisper in his ear. Say, "He (she) is telling a very good story." / Have that other person nod his head. / Have the story end. / Have the audience clap. / Be in the audience clapping for yourself up on the stage.

Be up on the stage. / Bow to the audience. / Have them clap. / Whistle a tune for them. / Have them clap. / Sing a song for them. / Have them cheer. / Run around the stage and turn handsprings for them. / Have them stamp their feet and cheer. / Whistle another tune for them. / Have them tell you to stop. / Sing them another song. / Have them tell you to go away. / Turn handsprings for them. / Have them all walk out of the theater.

Have new people there. / Recite for them. / Have them all walk out of the theater. / Whistle at them. / Have all the people come running back and sit down in the seats. / Say

"Gobble-gobble-gobble!" to them. / Have them clap and cheer and stamp their feet and tell each other that you are wonderful.

What would you like to do for them now? / All right. / Is there anything else you would like to do? / All right. / Is there anything else you would like the audience to do? / All right.

What was the name of the game we just played?

# Captive

*People like to move around when they want to. They like to feel free. They don't want to be tied up, or locked up, or sat on. Sometimes they don't even want to sit still in a chair. Do you feel like that sometimes? I feel like that sometimes.*

This game is called CAPTIVE.

Let us imagine that we have a canary in a cage. / Turn him green. / Turn him blue. / Have him jumping around inside the cage. / Have him wishing he could fly outside. / Have him open the door of the cage and fly out. / Have him fly around the room. / Have him be glad to be outside. / Have him fly back into the cage. / Have him shut the door.

Put a lock on the door. / Have the canary try to open the door. / Have him stay in the cage, crying. / Have him stamp and shout. / Have him roll on the floor of the cage because he is so angry. / Have him jump up and bend the bars of the cage apart. / Have him fly out into the room. / Have him fly around the room, singing. / Have him fly back into the cage. / Have him bend the bars back into place again.

Now you be inside the cage instead of the canary. / Jump around inside the cage. / Try to get out of the cage. / Bend the bars of the cage and jump out. / Grow bigger. / Take the cage apart and throw the pieces away.

Have a new cage, big enough for you. / Be inside it. / Bend the bars and jump out. / Grow even bigger. / Take the new cage apart and throw the pieces away.

Be inside an old castle. / Be locked in a dungeon at the bottom of the castle. / Have the dungeon made of stone, with iron bars. / Wish that you could be outside. / Put your hand against the wall of the dungeon and push the wall out into the moat. / Jump out of the dungeon. / Put your hand against the castle wall and push just a little. / Have the whole castle fall down with a great crash. / Put a new castle there. / Take a deep breath and blow the new castle down. / Blow all the pieces away. / Put a new castle there. / Put nothing there. / Look all around and see that there is no castle there.

Be in a cave. / Have many big rocks fall down outside and cover up the entrance of the cave. / Walk all around the cave and find that there is no way out. / Take a little breath and puff all the rocks away from the entrance of the cave. / Put new rocks there. / Put no rocks there. / Look at the entrance of the cave and see that there are no rocks there. / Walk out of the cave into the sunlight. / Look back at the cave. / Frown at the cave. / Have the cave fall flat. / Have flowers grow up out of the flat cave.

Be all tied up with thick ropes. / Have them around your wrists, and arms, and legs, and stomach, and feet. / Have them tight. / Lie there for a long time, all tied up. /

Wonder if anyone is going to come and set you free. / Decide that no one is going to come. / Take a deep breath and break all the ropes. / Burn the ropes in a furnace. / Look around and see that there are no ropes.

Be sitting in a chair. / Have iron bands holding you in the chair. / Have them around your wrists, and ankles, and chest, and neck. / Have someone telling you that you have to sit in that chair forever. / Yawn a great big yawn, and have the iron bands fall off. / Get up out of the chair. / Have the other person be very angry. / Take the chair apart and throw the pieces away. / Have the other person jump up and down in a rage.

Have another chair with iron bands. / Put that other person in it and fasten the iron bands. / Tell the other person to sit there for a week. / Have him (her) do it. / Unfasten the iron bands. / Let him (her) go free. / Take the chair apart and throw the pieces away. / Look around and see that there is no chair.

Where would you like to be now? / All right, be there. / Where now? / All right.

Look up in that corner of the room *(pointing)* and see that you are not up there. / Look in another place and see that you are not there. / Another place. / Another place.

What was the name of the game we just played?

# Hungry

*Would you be unhappy if you were hungry and had nothing at all to eat? I would. Would you like it if someone told you that you had to eat, when you were not hungry? I wouldn't. The best thing is to have just enough, isn't it?*

This game is called HUNGRY.

Let us imagine some things about being hungry and being not-hungry.

Let us imagine that we have a plate full of good things to eat. / Let us have a child looking at the plate. / You be the child. / Be hungry and want to eat the food. / Eat the food. / Throw the plate away. / Have another plate of food. / Want to eat it. / Eat the food. / Throw the plate away. / Have another plate of food. / Be not-hungry. / Throw the plate and the food away. / Have another plate of food. / Be not-hungry. / Throw it all away.

Have an empty plate. / Be hungry. / Wish you had something on the plate. / Have one bean on the plate. / Eat the one bean. / Be very hungry. / Have another bean on the plate. / Eat the bean. / Be very, very hungry. / Have another bean on the plate. / Eat the bean. / Be not-hungry. / Throw the plate away.

Have a room full of food. / Be not-hungry. / Begin to eat the food. / As you eat, get hungrier. / When you have eaten all the food, be the most hungry. / Have one bean. / Eat it. / Be not-hungry. / Have a mountain of food. / Begin to eat the mountain of food and get hungrier as you eat it. / When it is all gone, be the most hungry. / Have one grain of rice. / Eat the rice. / Be not-hungry.

Be at the table with Mother and Father. / Have three plates full of food. / Eat your food. / Eat Mother's food. / Eat Father's food. / Have Mother and Father be very hungry. / Throw away the plates and tell them there is no food.

Be at the table with them again. / Eat up all their food. / Tell them there is no more food. / Have them begin to cry.

Be at the table with them again. / Have them be not-hungry. / Tell them to eat their food. / Have them eat it. / Give them new plates of food. / Tell them to eat it. / Have them eat it. / Have them say they are really not-hungry now. / Give them new plates of food. / Have them eat it. / Have them swell up because of all the food they have eaten. / Have them say they cannot eat another bite. / Give them new plates of food. / Have them eat it. / Have them swell up as big as elephants. / Give them new plates. / Have them eat. / Have them swell up as big as a house. / Give them new plates. / Have them eat. / Have them swell up as big as a mountain. / Give them new plates. / Have them eat. / Have them swell up as big as the whole world. / Tell them they are a good Mother and Father for eating all their food.

Have them be thin again. / Have them be hungry. / Have a room full of food with things they like on one side, and things they don't like on the other side. / You eat all the good things. / Have Mother and Father eat all the things they don't like.

Have another room full of food. / Open the window and throw all the food out. / Have Mother and Father come in and ask for something to eat. / Tell them the food is all gone.

Have a room full of food. / Be very fat. Eat up all the food and grow thin. / Have no food. / Go a whole year without eating, and get fatter and fatter all the time.

Be very hungry. / Eat up all the food in the house. / Eat up all the suits and hats. / Eat up all the shoes and underwear. / Eat up all the furniture. / Eat up all the books. / Eat up all the windows and doors. / Eat up the roof. / Eat up the walls. / Eat up the floors. / Eat up all the trees around the house. / Eat up all the other houses. / Eat up all the mountains. / Eat up all the rivers. / Eat up all the oceans. / Eat up the whole world. / Be hungry still.

Have one bean. / Eat it up. / Be not hungry.

What would you like to do about that now? / All right.

What was the name of the game we just played?

# Mirror

*When you look straight into a mirror, you see your reflection. Your reflection looks just like you. What would it be like if your reflection looked bigger than you, or smaller, or looked like somebody else?*

This game is called MIRROR.

Imagine that you are standing in front of a big mirror. / You are looking at your reflection, and it is looking at you. / You smile at it, and it smiles at you. / You frown at it, and it frowns at you. / You nod your head at it, and it nods its head at you.

Now you smile at your reflection, but it frowns at you. /
You frown at it, and it smiles at you. / You nod your head
at it, and it shakes its head at you.

Have your reflection grow bigger, while you stay the way
you are. / You grow as big as your reflection. / Have your
reflection grow smaller, while you stay the way you are. /
You grow as small as your reflection. / Be your regular
size, but have your reflection be smaller than you. / Have
your reflection say, "I wish I could be as big as you are." /
Tell your reflection to get bigger. / Have it grow as big as
you are.

Look away from the mirror. / Look back and see that your
reflection has the head of a bear. / Look away. / Look
back and see that it is a whole bear. / Have it turn into a
girl (boy) *(opposite sex)*. / Have it turn into a boy (girl)
*(same sex)*. / Have your reflection look like you. / Have it
look like somebody else. / Whom does it look like?

Have it look like Father. / Have it look like Mother. / Have
it look like a teacher. / Which teacher does it look like? /
Have it look like an animal. / What animal does it look

like? / Have it look like a tree. / Have it look like a rock. / Have it look like a chair.

Have it look like some clothes standing there with nobody in them. / Have somebody in them. / Who is it? / Have your reflection look like you.

What would you like to have your reflection do now? / All right. / What now? / All right. / (Continue until the child runs out of ideas.)

What was the name of the game we just played?

# Manners

---

*Parents try to teach children good manners, but there are still a lot of bad manners around. Where do they come from? Do you suppose there is someone who is teaching the children bad manners? Who could it be?*

This game is called MANNERS.

Let us have a boy (girl) who has very bad manners. / Have him (her) teach his (her) parents to have bad manners. / Have him teach them to slam doors. / Have him teach them to break windows. / Have him teach them to shout at the dinner table. / Have him teach them to throw butter at each other. / Have him teach them to spill their milk. / Have him teach them to eat with their fingers. / Have him teach them to roll under the table. / Have him teach them to jump on top of the table and dance.

Have him teach them to interrupt each other. / Have him teach them to shout at guests. / Have him teach them to take the biggest piece of pie before anyone else can get it. / Have him teach them to do something else which is bad manners. / Have him teach them to do something else which is bad manners. / Something else which is bad manners.

Have a boy (girl) who has good manners. / Have him (her) teach his (her) parents to have good manners. / Have him teach them to close doors quietly. / Have him teach them to take good care of windows. / Have him teach them to speak softly at the table. / Have him teach them to use butter only as food. / Have him teach them to handle things without spilling them. / Have him teach them to eat with their forks and spoons. / Have him teach them to keep their napkins in their laps. / Have him teach them to stay in their chairs.

Have him teach them to listen to each other without interrupting. / Have him teach them to treat guests nicely. / Have him teach them to share good things fairly. / Have him teach them to do something else which is good manners. / Have him teach them to do something else which is good manners. / Something else which is good manners.

What would you like him (her) to teach them about manners now? / All right. / What now? / Is there anything else? / All right. / Is there anything you want to say about manners?

What was the name of the game we just played?

# Breathing

*When we breathe — like this* (demonstrate, in and out, mouth closed) *— the air goes in and out. If there is dust floating in the air, it goes in, too. Most of it sticks in your nose. If you get too much, you sneeze, or cough, or blow your nose.*

This game is called BREATHING.

Let us imagine that we have a goldfish in front of us. / Have the fish swim around. / Have the fish swim into your mouth. / Take a deep breath and have the fish go down into your lungs, into your chest. / Have the fish swim around in there. / Let out your breath and have the fish swim out into the room again.

Now breathe in a lot of tiny goldfish. / Have them swim around in your chest. / Breathe them all out again.

Let's see what kind of things you can breathe in and out of your chest. / Breathe in a lot of rose petals. / Breathe them out again. / Breathe in a lot of water. / Have it gurgling in your chest. / Breathe it out again. / Breathe in a lot of dry leaves. / Have them blowing around in your chest. / Breathe them out again. / Breathe in a lot of raindrops. / Have them pattering in your chest. / Breathe them out again. / Breathe in a lot of sand. / Have it blowing around in your chest. / Breathe it out again. / Breathe in a lot of little firecrackers. / Have them all popping in your chest. / Breathe out the smoke and bits of them that are left. / Breathe in a lot of little lions. / Have them all roaring in your chest. / Breathe them out again.

Breathe in some fire. / Have it burning and cracking in your chest. / Breathe it out again. / Breathe in some logs of wood. / Set fire to them in your chest. / Have them roaring as they burn up. / Breathe out the smoke and ashes.

Have a big tree in front of you. / Breathe fire on the tree and burn it all up. / Have an old castle in front of you. / Breathe fire on the castle and have it fall down. / Have an ocean in front of you. / Breathe fire on the ocean and dry it up.

What would you like to breathe in now? / All right. / Now what? / All right. / What would you like to burn up by breathing fire on it? / All right. / *(Continue these until the child runs out of ideas.)*

Be a fish in the ocean. / Breathe the water of the ocean, in and out. / How do you like that? / Be a bird high in the air. / Breathe the cold air, in and out. / How do you like that? / Be a camel on the desert. / Breathe the hot wind of the desert, in and out. / How does that feel? / Be an old-fashioned steam locomotive. / Breathe out steam and smoke all over everything. / How is that? / Be a stone. / Don't breathe. / How do you like that? / Be a boy (girl). /

Breathe the air of this room in and out. How do you like that?

What is the name of this game?

# Tick-Tock

*Do you know where your heart is? Yes. It beats all the time. It works like a pump. It makes the blood go. Sometimes fast. Sometimes slow. Most of the time we forget all about it.*

This game is called TICK-TOCK.

Let us imagine that you have a mechanical clock in your chest. / Let us hear it going "ticktock." / Have it on the right side. / Have it on the left. / Have it in the middle. / Have it right there *(pointing to the heart)*.

Have the clock right where your heart is. / Have it in your head. / Have it in your foot. / Have it out in the yard. / Have it in a clock shop. / Leave it there. / Turn your heart into a clock. / Have it go "tick-tock." / Have it run fast. / Have it run slow. / Have it run just right. / Throw it away. / Have a little sewing machine there, instead. / Have it run fast. / Have it run slow/ Have it run just right. / Throw it away. / Have a water pump there. / Have it pump fast. / Have it pump slow. / Have it pump at just the right speed. / Throw it away.

Have a balloon there. / Have it get bigger and bigger. / Have it pop. / Have a football there. / Have it get bigger. / Have it pop, too. / Have a firecracker there. / Light it. / Have it explode. / Have a light bulb there. / Light it. / Have it get hotter and hotter. / Have it melt. / Have a bomb there. / Have it explode.

Have your heart there. / Have it pump fast. / Have it pump slow. / Have it pump just right.

Have a lot of green dogs running around in your chest. / Have them running through your heart. / Have them turn yellow. / Throw them away. / Have a lot of men on horseback riding around in your chest. / Have them swinging swords. / Have them ride through your heart. / Have them slice it all up with their swords. / Throw away the horsemen. / Throw away the pieces of your heart. / Have a new heart.

Have it turn to gold. / Have it feel happy. / Have it turn to lead. / Have it feel sad. / Have it turn to wood. / Have it feel angry. / Have it turn to stone. / Have it feel cold. / Have it turn into a potato. / Have it turn to glass. / Have it turn into a piece of ice. / Throw it away. / Have a new heart.

Have it beat fast. / Have it beat slow. / Have it go just right. / What are you going to do with it now? / All right.

What was the name of this game?

# Camera

---

*Your head is something like a camera. The light goes into it at the front. The pictures are at the back. A camera is mostly empty, but your head isn't. A camera doesn't think, but you do. You know when you are looking at a camera, but a camera doesn't know when it is looking at you.*

This game is called CAMERA.

Let us imagine that your head is a camera, with two glass lenses in front, for eyes. / Open the lenses. / Close them.

/ Open them again. / Throw them away. / Have two new lenses. / Close them. / Open them. / Throw them away. / Have two new lenses.

Throw the lenses on the ground and stamp on them. / Have two new ones. / Throw those into the ocean. / Have two new ones. / Throw those into the fire. / Have two new ones. / Close them. / Open them.

Turn the camera into a head. / Have two eyes in front. / Close them. / Open them. / Throw them away. / Have two new ones. / Throw them on the ground and stamp on them. / Have two new ones. / Throw them into boiling water. / Have two new ones. / Throw them into the fire. / Have two new ones. / Make them beautiful. / Open them. / Close them.

Have your eyes turn to stone. / Have them turn to ice. / Have them be glowing coals. / Have them be glass. / Throw them away. Have new ones.

Have two little automobiles out in front of you. / Have them drive into your eyes. / Have two moons. / Push them into your eyes. / Have two suns. / Push them into your eyes. / Have two more suns. / Push them into your eyes. / Have two very big bright suns. / Push them into your eyes, too.

Have two new eyes. / Make them beautiful. / Close them. / Open them. / Blink them. / Have them feel happy.

Have two new eyes. / Have everything look green through them. / Have everything look yellow. / Have everything look dim, so that you cannot see things very well. / Have everything look bright and clear, so that you can see things perfectly. / Have everything look upside down. / Have everything look right side up again.

Have a man who is blind. / Give him two new eyes. / Have a woman who is blind. / Give her two new eyes. / Have a boy who is blind. / Give him new eyes. / Have a girl who is blind. / Give her new eyes. / Have a baby whose eyes hurt. / Give the baby new eyes. / Is there anyone else you would like to give new eyes to? / All right. / Anyone else? / All right.

What would you like to do about eyes now? / All right.

What was the name of this game?

# All Over

*When do you think about your stomach? Most of us think about our stomachs only when they hurt. Is that fair? Suppose you were a stomach, and nobody thought about you unless you hurt. Let's make up for that right now.*

The name of this game is ALL OVER.

Fill your head full of water. / Have the water spray out of your ears. / Have it spray out of your nose. / Have it spray out of your eyes. / Have it spray out of your mouth. / Have the water go back into your ears. / Have it go back into your nose. / Have it go back into your eyes. / Have it go back into your mouth. / Have it spray out of all those places again.

Have a fire in your stomach. / Have your stomach full of ice. / Have it full of hot cereal. / Have it full of water. / Have it full of nothing. / Have it full of ice cream. / Have it full of sand. / Have nothing in it at all. / Have no stomach. / Have a new stomach. / What do you want to do about your stomach now? / All right.

Have your backbone get hot. / Have it get cold. / Have it get soft. / Have it get hard. / Have it turn blue. / Have it turn white. / Have it turn any color you like. / Take it out and throw it away. / Have a new backbone. / Have it crooked. / Have it straight. / Take it out. / Tie it in a bow. / Throw it away. / Have a new one. / Have it come apart and fall on the floor in pieces. / Have a new backbone. / What do you want to do with it? / All right.

Have your skin be cold. / Have it be hot. / Have it turn blue. / Have it turn green. / Have it turn to wood. / Have it get furry. / Have it grow scales like a fish. / Have it grow feathers. / Have it get smooth. / Have it be beautiful. /

Have it get sores all over. / Have it be smooth again. / Have it feel good. / Have it itch. / Have it burning with fire all over. / Have it all burn up. / Have new skin. / Have it soft and smooth. / Have it tough as leather. / Have it hard as rock. / Have it soft and smooth. / How do you want it now? / All right.

What was this game called?

# Boo!

Most children are a little bit afraid of the dark. I was afraid of the dark when I was a child. Children think that something may be hiding in the dark, when nothing is really there. Or they think the chair is a bear, when it is really a chair. Sometimes even grown-ups feel that way, but not so often as children do.

This game is called BOO!

Be asleep. / Be awake. / Be pretending to be asleep. / Be asleep. / Be awake. / Be asleep.

Be afraid of me. / Be not-afraid of me. / Be afraid of the table. / Be not-afraid of the table.

Is there something else you want to be afraid of? / All right, be afraid of it. / Now be not-afraid of it. *(Continue with this, until the child runs out of ideas.)*

Have a closet with the door shut. / Be outside the closet. / Have something scary in the closet. / Open the door and shout "Boo!" at the thing. / Have the thing be afraid of you. / Have it run away. / Have another closet. / Have a scary thing in it. / Open the door and shout "Boo!" / Have the thing run away.

Would you like to scare something else? *(If the answer is No, repeat the above paragraph. Then, skip this paragraph. If the answer is Yes, continue.)* What would you like to scare? / All right. / What else? / All right. *(Continue until the child runs out of ideas.)*

What would you like to do about scaring now? / All right.

What is this game called?

128  *BOO!*

# Squeeze

---

*A thimble is a little metal cap that goes on your finger. When you are sewing, you use the thimble to push the needle through the cloth. If you look inside a thimble, you can see that it is not big enough to hold very much.*

This game is called SQUEEZE.

Have a thimble. / Take a big automobile and squeeze it into the thimble. / Take a tree and squeeze it into the thimble, too. / Squeeze a house into the thimble. / Squeeze a mountain in, with all the other things. / How is the thimble? Not full yet? / Squeeze the moon into the thimble. / Squeeze the sun into the thimble. / Squeeze the stars into the thimble. / How is it? Is it full now? / Do you want to squeeze anything else into it? / All right.

Take a horse and put him in your closet. / Have an elephant in your bed. / Have a steamroller in the bathroom. / Have a giraffe in a milk bottle. / Have a lion in a matchbox.

Have a battleship in your pocket. / Have a thimble in your hand. / Have everything in the whole world in the thimble. / Squeeze it.

What would you like to put into it now? / All right. / Anything else? / All right.

What is this game called?

# Being Things

*If you have bad manners, you may eat like a pig, but you can't really be a pig. You can't know how a pig feels. The best way to imagine how a pig feels is to imagine that you are a pig. You can say, "Now I am a pig." There is nothing you can't be, in your imagination.*

Would you like to be some things? / All right, this game is called BEING THINGS.

Be a bird. / Be a dog. / Be a pig. / Be an eagle. / Be a duck. / Be a tiger. / Be a lizard. / Be a shark. / Be a giraffe. / Be a chicken. / Be a mosquito. / Be a tarantula.

/ Be a rattlesnake. / Be an octopus. / Be a whale. / Be a goldfish in a bowl. / Be a cat. / Be a horse. / Be an ant. / Be a bee. / Be a butterfly. / Be a black widow spider. / Be a tree. / Be a squirrel. / Be a rabbit. / Be a wolf. / Be a hawk. / Be a pelican.

What is the most awful thing to be that you can think of? / All right, be that. / Now be the nicest thing you can think of. / Be something else. / Be something else.

Be something standing still. / Be something moving. / Be something walking. / Be something swimming. / Be something flying. / Be something lying down. / Be something standing up.

Be something hot. / Be something cold. / Be a mountain. / Be a person. / Be young. / Be old. / Be a tree. / Be a house. / Be a stone. / Be an animal. / Be a fish. / Be a snake. / Be a bird. / Be an insect. / Be water. / Be earth. / Be fire. / Be air. / Be wind, blowing. / Be a doughnut. / Be the hole in the doughnut. / Be an empty bottle. / Be the space in the bottle. / Be a balloon. / Be the air in the balloon.

Be Mother. / Be yourself. / Be Father./ Be yourself . / Be Brother. / Be yourself. / Be Sister. / Be yourself. / Be Uncle. / Be yourself. / Be Aunt. / Be yourself. / Be a doctor. / Be yourself. / Be a nurse. / Be yourself. / Be a policeman. / Be yourself.

Who would you like to be now? / All right. / Anyone else? / All right.

Be a rock. / Be a mountain. / Be the moon. / Be the sun. / Be a star. / Be an airplane, flying. / Be an automobile. / Be a boat. / Be a telephone. / Be a letter. / Be a volcano. / Be a white cloud. / Be a black cloud. / Be yourself. / Be something no one has ever been before. / What is it?

Be nothing. / Be something. / Be nothing. / Be something.

What would you like to be now? / All right.

What is this game called?

# Heavy

*If you throw a baseball or a stone back over your shoulder, will it break a window? Or hit somebody? It might. It would be dangerous to throw an automobile back over your shoulder. Better not do that. Not a real one.*

This game is called HEAVY.

Let us imagine that you are walking down the street. / Lean down and pick up a penny. / Throw it over your shoulder. / Pick up a baseball. / Throw it over your shoulder. / Pick up a watermelon and throw it over your shoulder. / Hear it break when it hits the street. / Look back and see the seeds scattered all over.

Pick up a suitcase and throw it over your shoulder. / Pick up a horse that is standing there and throw it over your shoulder. / Pick up an automobile and throw it over your shoulder. / Pick up a truck and throw it over your shoulder.

Walk up to an office building, ten stories high. / Take hold of the handles of the front door. / Pick the whole building up by its door handles. / Throw it over your shoulder.

Lean down and try to pick up a toy dog. / Have the dog be too heavy to pick up. / Have two big men trying to pick the dog up, but have it be too heavy. / Have a machine trying to pick the dog up, but have it be too heavy. / You pick up the dog. / Have the dog kiss you.

Now, walk up to Father and pick him up with one hand. / Pick Mother up with the other hand. / While you are holding them, have Father pick up a policeman. / Have Mother pick up a nurse. / You walk around, holding them all up. / Have them say, "Put us down. Put us down." / Put them down. / Have them say, "Thank you."

What would you like to pick up now? / All right. / What now? / All right.

What was the name of the game we just played?

# Baby

*Babies have a pretty good time. People are always picking them up and carrying them around. Or giving them baths and changing their diapers. Or feeding them. Or kissing them and rocking them to sleep. Suppose there were a very big baby who could pick people up.*

This game is called BABY.

Be a baby. / Have Mother holding you in her arms. / Have Father come up and say, "Let me hold the baby." / Have Mother say, "No, the baby belongs to me." / Have Father say, "Please let me hold the baby." / Have Mother give you to Father to hold.

Have Father rock you in his arms and sing you a song. / Have Mother come up and say, "Please let me hold the baby." / Have Father say, "Do I have to?" / Have Mother say, "Yes, I want the baby." / Have Father give you to Mother to hold.

Have a big baby who is holding Mother and Father in his (her) arms. / Have him (her) rock them and sing them a song. / Have the baby tell them that he (she) loves them. / Have the baby tell them to go to sleep. / Have them go to sleep.

What would you like the baby to do now? / All right. / What now? / All right. *(Continue until the child runs out of ideas.)*

What was the name of the game we just played?

# **Hard**

---

*When we walk around, we are walking through air. You can't see it, but if you swing your hand around, you can feel it. Air is easy to walk through. At the beach or in a swimming pool you can walk through water. Water is harder to walk through than air. Trees or bricks or rocks are too hard to walk through, except in your imagination.*

This game is called HARD.

Be outdoors, walking. / Walk through some tall grass. / Walk through some bushes. / Walk up to a thick hedge. /

Walk right through it. / Walk up to a big tree trunk. / Walk right through it.

Find a big rock. / Walk into the middle of it and look around inside it. / Have it look rocky in there. / Walk out on the other side of the rock. / Walk up to a brick wall. / Walk through it. / Walk through a stone wall. / Walk through an automobile. / Walk through a railroad engine.

Be up in an airplane, flying around the world. / Jump out of the airplane. / Start to fall down to the ground. / Wonder whether you are going to hit hard when you land. / Be afraid. / Decide that you are going to fall right through the world. / When you get to the ground, fall right through the world and come out the other side. / Now fall back to the ground on the other side of the world. / This time, hit hard when you land. / Have the world say, "Ouch!" / Say, "I'm sorry." / Have the world say, "That's all right."

Be walking along by the side of a road. / Have your feet start to sink into the ground. / Sink in up to your knees, but keep on walking. / Sink in up to your waist. / Sink in up to your chest, and keep on walking. / Sink in up to your chin. / Sink all the way in. / Keep on walking.

Walk by some big rocks, under the ground. / Walk by some water pipes down there. / Look at them and see how rusty they are. / Walk under the road. / Listen to the cars rumbling along, up above you.

Walk away from the road until you are under a grassy field. / Walk by the roots of a big tree. / Listen to a gopher working in his burrow. Hear him go *scratch, scratch, scratch.* / Poke a hole in his burrow, so that you can talk to him. / Say, "Hello, gopher." / Have the gopher say, "What are you doing down here?" / Tell him you are exploring. / Have him say, "Okay."

Walk under a hill. / Find a big cave. / Walk into the cave. / Walk toward the mouth of the cave. / Walk out of the cave onto the grassy field. / Look all around at the trees and bushes. / Dust your clothes off. / Take a deep breath. / Have the air smell good. / Notice that the gopher is looking at you out of his hole. / Say, "Goodbye, gopher." / Have him say goodbye.

What would you like to do about those things now? / All right.

What was the name of the game we just played?

# Seeing

When you lose something, do you run all around looking for it? That is one way to find it. Another way is to stay where you are and look into all the places where it might be. You are not looking with your eyes but with your memory and your imagination. Often you can find what you have lost right away. Of course, it doesn't always work — but then running all around doesn't always work, either.

This game is called SEEING.

Let us imagine that you can see anywhere. / Look into the next room and see what is in there. / Look into the next house. / What do you see? / Look into another house. /

What do you see? / Look into a store. / What do you see? / Look into another store. / What do you see?

Look inside a clock. / See the wheels going around. / Look under a bed. / See someone's shoe that is lost under there. / Look into a dark closet. / See the clothes hanging there. / Look into the ocean. / See the fish swimming there. / Look into the sand at the beach. / See a box buried there. / Look into the box. / See gold coins and pearls and rubies and diamonds and emeralds and candy inside the box.

Be in your bed at night. / Have the room be all dark. / Look at everything in the room. / Have it easy to see all the things in the room, even though the room is dark. / What do you see in your dark room? / What else? / What else? *(Continue until the child runs out of ideas.)*

Look into a can of beans that Mother has left in your dark room by mistake. / Have the beans say, "Shhh!" / Ask them, "What are you doing in my dark room?" / Have them say, "Sleeping, silly."

What would you like to look into now? / All right. / What now? / All right.

What was the name of the game we just played?

# Ouch

*When you go to the doctor and he says, "This won't hurt,"*
*what usually happens? Sometimes he says, "This may hurt*
*a little bit." Then what happens? Sometimes when we think*
*we are going to be hurt, we say "Ouch!" before anything*
*hurts us. Have you done that? I've done that.*

This game is called OUCH!

Imagine that you are running after a ball. / Fall down and
bump your knee. / Have it hurt. / Say "Ouch!" / Now run
again, but don't fall down. / Have your knee hurt anyway.

/ Say "Ouch!" / Run again, fall down, and bump your knee. / Have it not hurt at all. / Say "Ouch!"

Have another boy (girl) who is running after a ball. / Have him (her) fall down and bump his (her) knee. / Feel the hurt in your own knee. / Say "Ouch!"

*(Repeat this paragraph twice, using first the opposite sex, then the same sex.)*

Now be at the doctor's office. / Have the doctor say he is going to give you a shot. / Have him say, "This won't hurt." / Have him give you the shot. / Have it hurt. / Say "Ouch!" / Have the doctor say, "That didn't hurt."

Tell the doctor you are going to give him a shot. / Tell him it won't hurt. / Give him the shot. / Have it hurt him. / Have him say "Ouch!" / Tell him it didn't hurt you. / Have him say, "But it hurt *me*."

Be at school. / Tell the teacher about your shot. / Show the place to the teacher. / Have the place hurt. / Say "Ouch!"

/ Have the teacher ask, "Why did you say 'Ouch'?" / Say, "Because my shot hurt."

Now I want you to do something really. Put your hand on your head and say "Ouch!" / Very good. / Now put your hand on your knee and say "Ouch!" / Now the other knee. / Good.

Each thing I name, you put your hand on it and say "Ouch!" / Ready? Here we go.

Your head. / Your knee. / Your other knee. / Your other hand. / Your shoulder. / Your nose. / Your ear. / Your other ear. / The back of your neck. / The top of your head. / Your chin. / Your chest. / Your stomach. / Your leg. / Your other leg. / Your knee. / Your other knee. / Your foot. / Your other foot. / Your back. / All right.

What would you like to say "Ouch!" about now? / (*Let the child say "Ouch!" or talk about ouches until he runs out of ideas.*)

What was the name of the game we just played?

# Bed

*We don't like to feel sick, but sometimes we like to stay in bed to read a book, or sleep, or watch television, or do something else. Sometimes we like to stay in bed because we don't feel like going to school. After a while, we get tired of staying in bed, and we want to get up.*

This game is called BED.

Let us imagine that you are staying home from school and are in bed for the day. / Have Mother come in and ask how you are feeling. / Tell her you feel fine. / Have her take your temperature. / Have her say, "Your temperature is normal." / Have her give you some good medicine. /

Have her bring you all the things you want to eat and drink. / Have her read to you. / Have her play games with you. / Tell her you want to get up. / Have her say, "If you can get up, you can go to school." / Tell her you will stay in bed and not go to school.

Have Mother take you to see the doctor. / Have the doctor look into your ears. / Have him put a cold stethoscope on your chest and listen to your breathing. / Have him look into your throat. / Have him push your tongue down with a stick. / When he does that, you say, "Aggle, aggle, aggle!" / Have him say, "This child is not sick." / Have Mother take you toward school. / Tell her you would rather go home to bed. / Have her take you home and put you to bed. / Say "Thank you, Mother." / Have her say, "That is all right."

How long are you going to stay in bed like that? / What do you want to do there? / What else? (Continue until the child runs out of ideas.) / Do you want to get up now? / All right.

What was the name of the game we just played?

154   BED

# Here

---

*I am going to ask you where some things are. I want you to point to each thing as I ask about it.*

Where is your head? / Where is your foot? / Where is your hand? / Where is your stomach? / Where am I? / Where is the floor? / Where is the ceiling? / Where is the wall? / Where is your ear?

Where is your fist? / Where is your elbow? / Where is your shoulder? / Where is your chair?

Shake your head. / Move your foot. / Nod your head. /
Move your other foot. / Clap your hands. / All right.

*(Optional.)* Stand up. / Reach for the ceiling. / Put your
arms down. / Walk around your chair. / Sit down. / What
would you like to do now?

What was the name of the game we just played?

# Touch

*Now I am going to ask you to touch some things. Put your finger on each thing when I tell you.*

Touch the floor. / Touch the wall. / Touch the chair. / Touch the table. / Touch the bed *(or other object)*. / Touch the glass. / Touch the........../ Touch the........../ Touch the..........

Touch the window. / Touch the other side of the door.

What do you want to touch now? / All right.

# References

Adams, James L. *Conceptual Blockbusting*. San Francisco Book Co. 1976.

Brown, George I. *Human Teaching for Human Learning*. Viking-Compass 1972, Gestalt Journal Press 1990.

Bry, Adelaide & Marjorie Bair. *Directing the Movies of Your Mind: Visualization for Health and Insight*. Harper & Row 1978.

Castillo, Gloria A. *Left-Handed Teaching: Lessons in Affective Education*. Praeger 1974.

Dellas, Marie & E. M. Gaier. Identification of creativity. *Psychological Bulletin,* 1970, 73, 55-73.

Dunlap, Knight. *Habits: Their Making and Remaking*. Liveright 1932.

Farber, S. M. & R. H. L. Wilson, editors. *Control of the Mind*. McGraw-Hill 1961.

Guilford, J. P. *The Nature of Human Intelligence*. McGraw-Hill 1967.

Hammer, Max. The directed daydream technique. *Psychotherapy,* 1967, 4, 173-181.

Huxley, Aldous. *Island.* Harper & Row 1962.

Johnsgard, Keith W. Symbol confrontation in a recurrent nightmare. *Psychotherapy,* 1969, 6, 177-182.

Jung, Carl G. The structure of the unconscious. In *Two Essays on Analytical Psychology.* Meridian 1956.

Klinger, Eric. *Structure and Functions of Fantasy.* Wiley 1971.

Locke, Edwin A. Is "behavior therapy" behavioristic? *Psychological Bulletin,* 1971, 76, 318-327.

Maslow, A. H. *Motivation and Personality.* Harper 1954.

McKim, Robert H. *Experiences in Visual Thinking.* Brooks/Cole/Wadsworth 1972.

Perls, F. S. *Ego, Hunger & Aggression.* Durban 1942, Random House 1969, Gestalt Journal Press 1992. Part 3, Concentration Therapy: Visualisation.

————, R. F. Hefferline, & P. Goodman. *Gestalt Therapy: Excitement and Growth in the Human Personality.* Julian Press 1951, Gestalt Journal Press 1994.

Polanyi, Michael. *Personal Knowledge.* Harper & Row 1964.

Rachman, S. Systematic desensitization. *Psychological Bulletin,* 1967, 67, 93-103.

Sheehan, P. W. Functional similarity of imaging to perceiving. *Perceptual and Motor Skills,* 1966, 23, 1011-1013.

——, editor. *The Function and Nature of Imagery.* Academic Press 1972.

Singer, Jerome L. *Daydreaming.* Random House 1966.

——. Imagery and daydream techniques employed in psychotherapy. *Current Topics in Clinical and Community Psychology,* 1971, 3, 1-51.

——. *The Child's World of Make-Believe: Experimental Studies of Imaginative Play.* Academic Press 1973.

——. *The Inner World of Daydreaming.* Harper & Row 1975.

Wilkins, Wallace. Desensitization. *Psychological Bulletin,* 1971, 76, 311-317.

Yawkey, T. D., E. Askov, C. A. Cartwright, M. A. Dupuis, S. L. Fairchild, & M. L. Yawkey. *Language Arts and the Young Child.* Peacock 1981.